Literacy

Teaching Literacy

Using Texts to Enhance Learning

David Wray

 David Fulton Publishers

David Fulton Publishers Ltd
The Chiswick Centre, 414 Chiswick High Road, London W4 5TF

www.fultonpublishers.co.uk

First published in Great Britain in 2004 by David Fulton Publishers

10 9 8 7 6 5 4 3 2 1

Note: The right of David Wray to be identified as the author of this work has been asserted by him in accordance with the Copyright, Designs and Patents Act 1988.

David Fulton Publishers is a division of Granada Learning Limited, part of ITV plc.

Copyright © David Wray 2004

British Library Cataloguing in Publication Data
A catalogue record for this book is available from the British Library.

ISBN 1-85346-717-0

Typeset by FiSH Books, London
Printed and bound in Great Britain

Contents

This book is dedicated to Alexander, whose reactions to texts of all kinds have taught me what an engaging process literacy can be.

Introduction: Another book about teaching literacy?

Literacy and its teaching have to be the most widely written about, and researched, subjects in the whole of education. Each year, even in the United Kingdom, there are probably about two dozen new books published on these subjects, a figure that would be at least quadrupled if we also counted books published in the USA, and increased substantially again if the whole of the English-speaking world were included. This begs two questions: Why all those books; and Can a new book possibly have anything original to say about such well-worked themes?

The first question is relatively easy to answer. So much material is published about literacy teaching simply because the topic is of such burning interest and importance, not just to teachers and schools, but also to parents, and hence to politicians and the media. Whether true or not, the popular perception is that success in literacy is closely bound up with more general educational and life success. Everyone – from parent to employers, from teachers to the Chancellor of the Exchequer – has an interest in maximising the success in literacy achieved by young people. Highly literate youngsters achieve more in school, and they perform more effectively in the work place, benefiting their employers and paying more in tax. Levels of literacy are an issue of national importance.

Given such a high profile, it is hardly surprising that teachers, who have to produce these high outcomes, absorb new ideas and insights into the process of teaching literacy avidly. There are so many books published on the teaching of literacy simply because teachers buy, borrow and read them.

The second of the questions posed above is a little harder. Given that there is so much published material in the field, what fresh insights can a new book offer on this subject? In other words, why have I written this book? The answer to this question lies in the nature of developments in literacy teaching (particularly in England, although these issues have resonances across the globe) in the last six or seven years. These years have seen the introduction in England of a National Literacy Strategy which has provided a strong blueprint for literacy teaching, both at primary and secondary school levels, in this country. This strategy has had a number of very important effects. At one level it has undoubtedly contributed to a rise in teacher knowledge about, and skill in, teaching literacy, which has also had an effect in raising pupil achievement. Literacy teaching, particularly to junior pupils (Key Stage 2), is more systematic and structured. Teachers are much better at focusing lessons upon particular learning objectives and at developing achievable learning targets for groups of pupils as well as for individuals.

Yet it is this very targeting process wherein lies perhaps the biggest problem inherent in the Literacy Strategy, and in parallel developments elsewhere in the world, especially in the USA. When we continually break down the skills of literacy, we risk atomisation and forgetting that the wholeness of the process is what is important. Teaching pupils to read consonant digraphs, or to write effective story openings, or to recognise subordinate clauses in a sentence, are important skills, but only because they enhance pupils' reading and writing of whole, connected texts. Targeting specific literacy skills is only useful if it leads to pupils being able to use these skills in real, whole, literacy experiences. And the key factor in such whole experiences is the presence of a text.

Literacy is about texts: readers read texts, writers write texts. A text is a piece of connected language that serves a function in social interchange: it has purpose, it is constructed and exists within a social context and it implies dialogue. For every writer there is a reader, for every reader a writer. Texts communicate. It is my contention, and a major part of the rationale behind this book, that we have spent so much time recently taking literacy apart, that we have neglected its central feature – text.

This book, therefore, is about texts. More specifically, it is about how we might develop our pupils' abilities to understand, respond to, use, critique, create and construct texts for a wide range of purposes.

An overview of the book

The book begins with an attempt to put text at the heart of the literacy and literacy learning process. It suggests that text has often been placed in the role as servant to all kinds of teaching agendas, and its function as a vehicle for communication of meaning given too low a priority. A key step to take in raising this priority is to explore the interactions which take place between text and reader, which we usually refer to as 'understanding'.

The next chapter then takes up this idea and explores in more detail the nature of understanding a text, by examining some of the difficulties this may cause for less experienced readers. The crucial interactive (or 'transactional' in some writers' terminology) nature of understanding is stressed.

The following two chapters explore a range of ways in which teachers might respond to this view of understanding as an interaction between text and reader. Teaching strategies useful for both fiction and non-fiction texts are explored.

The focus then moves to the creation of text with an examination of how teachers might support and develop pupils' writing. The argument advanced here is that the teaching of the skills of writing is best carried out within the context of seeing writing as an apprenticeship in which novice writers learn from more experienced writers, like teachers. Many practical implications of this approach are developed.

Of course, writing does not simply get done in lessons called literacy or English. The texts pupils are expected to create during their school careers will cover a wide range of purposes and structures. Most teachers are aware of the role of writing in the 'literary' subjects – for example, English, history, and other social subjects. There is less certainty about the role of writing within the technical subjects – mathematics and science in particular. Accordingly, the next two chapters focus on writing in science and mathematics respectively, in each case taking a close look at the kinds of texts expected in these subjects before going on to make some suggestions about how writing might be taught in each context.

The texts which pupils come across in the world outside school will invariably have been written, explicitly or implicitly, to influence the views, ideas and feelings of their readers. The development of critical literacy is a crucial aspect to literacy development and the next chapter explores this in some detail, making a number of suggestions as to how teachers might deliberately teach a critical approach to texts.

The final two chapters focus on developments in the nature of text, in particular how pupils might be taught to read and write electronic texts.

Texts, literacy and learning

Introduction

All readers of this book will have at least one thing in common with the author. At some point in our lives we were all taught to read and to write. This teaching may have come from a person, or persons, or it may have been the result of particular experiences or environments. Yet taught we were, none of us being so fortunate as to be born literate. This observation sounds so obvious as to be trite, but it repays some thought as a starting point for a consideration of the teaching and learning of literacy.

Because most people, and, by definition, all those reading this book, are fairly accomplished readers, we tend to think very little about the ways in which we learnt this process and the teaching that we received. If we are asked to remember a time when we could not read, most of us have great difficulty in doing so. Being able to read seems so natural to us now that our acquisition of it is taken for granted.

The picture is similar when we think about our learning to write. Many people, when asked to think back to a time when they had difficulty in writing, will only refer to such experiences as being aware that they were untidy writers, or being unable to spell a word. These are only part of the writing process, of course. The more important aspect – understanding the purpose of making, and being able to make, meaningful symbols which can be read back – is often, like reading, taken for granted. Yet at some point in our lives all of us were given lengthy lessons, often repeated many times, in reading and writing. We were taught to read and write. What memories do we have of this teaching?

When I first meet groups of students, at the beginning of their initial teacher training courses, I always make a point of asking them to write about their memories of their own first encounters with reading and writing. This usually causes them some difficulty, and it will often take a little while before they realise that I am serious enough about the task for them to have to produce something. The written accounts that result from this task are then used as a starting point for a discussion about fundamentals in the learning of literacy. Remarkably, most accounts have a great deal in common with one another. Some concentrate upon early experiences of reading and two typical examples are given here:

> I don't remember much about reading in the infants' school. I think we used Peter and Jane. I remember getting very excited when I brought my first book home from the library. It was the story of Peter Rabbit and my mum had already read it to me at home. I insisted on reading it to Mum, Dad and my older brother that night before I would go to bed. I've still got a copy of that book, although the original fell apart through being read so much.

> I learnt to read by reading the instructions for my Meccano set. I wanted to build a crane and there was nobody to help me. I remember struggling with the instruction booklet until I managed to figure it out.

Other accounts concentrate upon writing, and again, two typical examples are given:

> I wrote a book when I was six. It was all about dinosaurs. We had been watching a television series at school and after each programme we had to copy out some notes from the blackboard. I decided to write about the programmes in my own words at home. My mother still has the book although it's a bit dog-eared now.

> We used to write stories at school. I liked to write about ghosts and monsters. I remember my teacher telling me that one of my stories was 'really gruesome' and I pretended to know what she meant. I got my Mum to help me find that word in the dictionary when I got home and the next day I told the teacher I was going to write another 'gruesome' story.

It is very noticeable from these accounts that what these students tend to remember seems not to be the experience of learning to read and write but rather the particular texts which they read or wrote. This anecdotal evidence of the influence of texts upon literate and proto-literate people fits with an increased recent emphasis upon the importance of text itself in the development of literacy. Until fairly recently, somewhat surprisingly, text, the essential material of literacy, had been rather neglected in research into, and developments in, literacy teaching. While it has become a focus of attention in the last few years, in the process several tensions have emerged which have caused debate among practitioners and researchers alike. Text is back on the agenda but in a fairly controversial way.

The literacy triangle

A model of the factors important in literacy teaching might be represented as a triangle with text at its centre (Figure 1.1). According to this model, basically, the teacher teaches the child to read and write in a particular instructional, usually classroom, context and using particular texts.

Our understandings about each of the parts of this model are now substantial. I will outline them briefly here.

The child as language learner and user

We now know a good deal about what reading and writing actually involve for the child and this emphasis upon the processes of literacy is in itself a significant shift from a previous concentration upon the products of reading and writing. We have learnt that the processes of reading and writing are complex and multi-dimensional and that they are influenced by, and to some extent depend upon, the purposes for which they are carried out. We also know that in learning these processes, children work out their own rules for how things work,

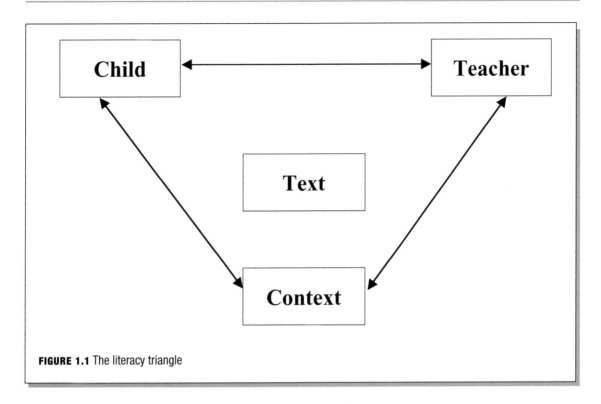

FIGURE 1.1 The literacy triangle

progressively refining these in the light of wider and wider experience. This realisation of the active role of the learner in the learning has taught us the importance of examining the perceptions children have about these processes and purposes of reading and writing (Medwell 1990; Wray 1994).

The role of the teacher

The role of the teacher has come under considerable scrutiny and it is possible to discern at least two distinct trends in thinking about this role. On the one hand, during the latter part of the twentieth century, there was a discernible shift in emphasis from foregrounding the teacher as an instructor to widening the role to include teacher as facilitator, teacher as audience, teacher as model and teacher as co-participant. This shift coincided with a reconception of the learning process as a social construction of knowledge, rather than the traditional transmission/reception of knowledge model. The upshot of this change was that more stress began to be placed upon teaching as providing appropriate conditions for learning (Cambourne 1988; Wray *et al.* 1989).

More recently, we have also seen a renewed emphasis upon the role of the teacher as instructor and have begun to understand the crucial characteristics of effective teaching and effective teachers of literacy (Wray *et al.* 2002) and to realise that effective teaching of literacy is always concerned not just with the content of what is being taught but also the context in which that content is set.

Contexts for learning

A great deal of emphasis has been placed upon contexts for learning, in the sense of the environments in which learning is set. Stress has been placed upon the provision of demonstrations of literacy, upon the creation of atmospheres in which children feel safe to learn through experimentation and in which they get regular practice of using literacy for real purposes, and upon the careful structuring of support for children ('scaffolding' in Bruner's terms) as they 'emerge into literacy'. The features of this environment for learning were summed up as 'conditions for learning' (Cambourne 1988), and such was the power of these ideas that it occasionally seemed that all teachers needed to do was to create a suitable context wherein children would 'just learn'. The reality is, of course, that the business of teaching is not so simple and it is likely that a suitable context is a necessary, but not sufficient, condition for the efficient learning of literacy. In any case, it is beginning to become apparent that appropriate contexts are not as easily created as that, or as unproblematic. If context is perceived as subjective rather than objective reality, as the work of Edwards and Mercer (1987) and Medwell (1991) suggest, then there will be as many contexts in each classroom as there are children. Creating contexts will be dependent upon the individual perceptions of the participants in those contexts, which complicates the issue greatly.

The central role of text

In the past there was a tendency to under-estimate the importance of the texts which are created and recreated in the process of becoming literate. Texts were often thought of as simple servants of other pedagogic priorities. This can be seen clearly in the changing nature of the texts produced for early readers. These have been written for a number of purposes:

- *To teach phonic rules.* This approach produced phonically regular texts, and texts were graded according to the supposed complexity of the phonic rules they exemplified. Extreme versions of this principle produced texts such as 'Can Dan fan Nan?', but there were other reading programmes, such as Joyce Morris's *Language in Action* (Morris 1984), in which phonic regularity was handled much more sensitively and authors managed to produce some quite readable early texts.

- *To teach specific words.* This produced limited vocabulary texts where words were repeated so often that children could hardly help but become increasingly familiar with them. Such limitation, of course, makes the production of meaningful text quite a tall order and, again, extreme versions of this kind of text are now thought of as laughable: 'Oh, oh, oh. Look, Jane. Look, look, look'. A great many reading programmes, however, including such very popular schemes as *Oxford Reading Tree*, use versions of this principle as one of their bases for producing texts.

- *To stress predictability in reading.* This produced texts in which repetition was at the level of the phrase or sentence rather than the word. Once a child had read one page of such a text, it required little fresh learning to read the following pages. Texts such as 'Along came a crab, a big blue crab. "Ho ho," said the octopus, "come and play with me." "Oh no," cried the blue crab, "you'll eat me for your tea." Along came a squid, a juicy, green squid. "Ho ho," said the octopus...' [etc.] (*The Greedy Grey Octopus*, Tadpole Books) were designed to actively encourage predictive reading. Many modern reading programmes include texts which are similar to this in design.

■ *To be decodable*. A decodable text is defined as containing a large proportion of words that could be expected to be decoded (pronounced) based on the phonics lessons already taught to a child. This concept has recently become important (and controversial) in the debate about teaching reading in the USA, where the governing bodies of both of the largest states, Texas and California, changed their requirements in the late 1990s for the reading programmes they were willing to support. Where previously they had supported only reading programmes which included authentic literature and predictable texts, they now insisted that 80 per cent (in Texas) or 75 per cent (in California) of the texts used with beginning readers should be decodable. Decodable texts have much in common with the previously mentioned phonically regular texts, and may include some equally meaningless passages. It is important to note, however, that their envisaged role in the teaching of reading is different. While the early phonically regular texts were envisaged as themselves accomplishing a good deal of the teaching of early reading, decodable texts are designed to be used after the phonics teaching has taken place as a means of giving children the opportunity to apply what they have learnt.

Such views of text as a means to an end can be contrasted with views of text itself as central to the process of becoming literate. Children read and write texts, teachers teach reading and writing with and through texts, and texts provide a context for understanding, creating and responding to themselves and other texts. Modern literary theory lays great stress upon the idea that texts are never autonomous entities but are rather 'intertextual constructs: sequences which have meaning in relation to other texts which they take up, cite, parody, refute, or generally transform' (Culler 1981: 38). It would be possible to conceive of literacy learning as being simply a matter of a progressive elaboration of textual and intertextual experience.

Attention to the nature and importance of text in its own right has stemmed from two quite distinct directions of interest which have, at times, seemed contradictory in their implications. One of these directions might be termed *structuralist* as it has involved the close analysis of the structure of texts, from a linguistic perspective, largely inspired by the work of Michael Halliday. Chapman (1983a, 1987), drawing upon the framework for linguistic cohesion put forward by Halliday and Hasan (1976), examines carefully the ways in which text is bound together and self-refers; in fact, what makes a particular text a unity and not merely a string of discrete sentences or words. Chapman (1983b) also investigates the degree to which young readers are aware of the range of cohesive ties present in texts and finds that their level of such awareness is a significant element in their development as readers. He suggests that there is a need to take this element of text firmly into account when planning effective teaching programmes.

Drawing upon the analysis of language by Halliday as social semiotic (Halliday 1978), the group of Australian researchers collectively known as 'genre theorists' looked closely at the ways in which text structures reflect a variety of social ways of making meaning (Halliday and Hasan 1989). They drew from this work the implication that, unless some attention was actually given to teaching children to operate effectively within the genre structures upon which society is based, children were at risk of being disenfranchised from large parts of wider social life (Martin 1989; Christie 1990).

The second direction from which interest in text has come might be termed *authenticist*, as it has emphasised the importance of 'real' texts, that is texts written for authentic purposes (as opposed to instructional purposes, such as reading scheme texts). Several notable education-alists (in particular Meek 1988) pointed out the ways in which authentic texts can teach readers many important lessons about reading. One of the major motivations underlying what was widely termed the 'real books movement' in teaching reading was the idea that authentic texts were superior to linguistically controlled scheme, or basal, texts. In writing, similarly, authenticity has loomed very large. The process writing approach, inspired by the work of Graves (1983), placed great emphasis upon children 'finding their own voices' and composing texts which had real importance to them.

The structuralist and authenticist ways of looking at text have seemed to be in opposition to each other with, at times, this opposition spilling over into direct confrontation and unhelp-ful polarity. Structuralist views have been caricatured as implying a return to dry, direct teaching of textual features, reviving suspicions about the effectiveness and lack of child-centredness of grammar exercises. Authenticist approaches, on the other hand, have been caricatured as being structureless and giving no attention at all to developing children's awareness of textual conventions. Both these criticisms rest, of course, upon misunder-standings, and their existence is perhaps more an expression of the long-standing clash of educational philosophy usually referred to as 'traditional versus progressive' than of any seri-ous attempt to come to terms with the differing perspectives.

In any case, the two positions do seem, potentially, to have much in common. In essence they are both concerned with children's responses to and production of 'real' texts. The genre theorists have continually emphasised that textual structures, and thus the teaching of them, only make sense within a context of meaning.

> A functional approach to language does not advocate teaching about language by handing down prescriptive recipes. Rather it is concerned with providing information about the development of effective texts for particular purposes, and providing it at the point of need within the context of real, purposeful language use.
>
> (Derewianka 1990: 5)

Both positions, therefore, emphasise purpose and meaning in literacy development.

They are both also concerned with increasing children's control over their reception and production of texts. For 'real books' and process-writing advocates, the issue of children's choice is in the foreground of their intentions. Only by being allowed to make choices about what they read and write, they argue, can children develop the personal investment in the processes of literacy that is essential if they are to engage in real learning of these processes. For structuralists, developing children's control over the ways text is used for particular purposes in society is one of the foundations of their arguments. 'To learn to recognise and create the various genres found in one's culture is to learn to exercise choices – choices in building and ordering different kinds of meaning and hence, potentially, choices in directing the course of one's life' (Christie 1990: 3).

Texts across the curriculum

Of course, the texts that pupils read and write in the portions of their school curricula that are labelled 'literacy' or 'English' make up only a small part of their total school textual experience. Texts have a role to play in virtually all areas of the school curriculum.

To illustrate this point, Table 1.1 shows some of the reading that pupils are expected to do in a range of school subjects. The reading tasks are taken directly from schemes of work for each subject published by the Qualifications and Curriculum Authority, and in each case the suggested work is intended for Year 7 pupils (11- to 12-year-olds).

TABLE 1.1 Reading expectations for Year 7 pupils

Subject	Reading task
Art	Ask pupils to work in groups to research buildings. Ask them to examine and discuss: how design might be linked to function; technological developments; fashion; local materials; cost and skills available: – how decorative features can be associated with the purpose of a building; – the use of different visual and tactile qualities in architecture, e.g. Islamic detail and decoration compared with the work of ancient Greece; – the use of other qualities, e.g. geometric and organic shapes; – how the circle and the sphere are used in buildings from different times and cultures. Encourage the pupils to spot connections and links between how information is presented in different forms. Ask pupils to use skimming, scanning, highlighting and note-making as appropriate to different texts and to use contents, index, glossary, key words, hotlinks, etc. in finding information.
Citizenship	Using material from newspapers and organisations such as the Howard League and the Prison Reform Trust, discuss issues surrounding the treatment of young people convicted of crimes.
Design Technology	Show the pupils how to research sources of information about materials/ingredients, e.g. databases, ingredients lists on packaging, advertisements for food products, to help them select appropriate materials/ingredients.
Geography	Provide a range of resources about the school's general locality, e.g. aerial photographs, advertisements from local newspapers, brochures from the local council. Ask them to use these and what they have learnt to persuade someone to come and live here.

History	Ask pupils to use evidence from the Domesday Book to write a report for the new king, William Rufus, using information from the Domesday Book to give him some idea about what goes on in English towns and villages. Explain that the king is particularly interested in the economy and taxation. Discuss the kind of information the king would want about his kingdom. Provide background information and some typical entries, translated into English and with technical terms simplified. Use local extracts where possible.
ICT	Discuss the different types of search mechanisms provided on CD-ROMs and within internet sites, e.g. the hierarchical structure of a contents facility, site or content 'maps', key word searches, indexes, free-text and Boolean searches. Ask the pupils to define the questions they would like to answer through their research. Ask the pupils to investigate their chosen sources and to use the different facilities to find suitable information to answer their questions.
RE	Give groups of pupils accounts of one or two particular incidents, e.g. Zacchaeus, when Jesus talked about justice. The groups read the text. They quickly identify: – what was unjust about things before Jesus intervened; – what Jesus' intervention was; – how the intervention showed the person justice.
Science	Show pupils evidence of the early observations made by Robert Hooke and others to illustrate how the development of the microscope changed the way in which scientists viewed the structure of living things. Ask pupils to find out how ideas developed. Provide opportunities for pupils to read different types of text, reminding them of ways of identifying key points, and to discuss findings in groups before reporting back to the whole class, e.g. using flow charts or a series of annotated diagrams.

Examination of these tasks reveals that the kinds of text that are used in each subject are very different, but that the key aspects of reading that pupils need in order to complete them have some similarities. For most reading tasks, pupils need to locate particular information within texts and, principally, they need to find a way of *understanding* this information. It is to the nature of this process of understanding that we now need to turn.

Conclusion

In this chapter I have tried to put forward a rationale for the central role of text in the learning and teaching of literacy. I placed this in a triangle of key factors influencing the teaching of literacy and suggested that our attention has, typically, always been focused upon issues such as the processes of literacy, the strategies used to teach pupils these and the contexts in which these strategies are employed. All these factors are important, but it is my contention that the factor at the heart of the process – the raw material of literacy, the text itself – has been somewhat neglected in our thinking and needs to be given a more central role. In the rest of the book I will explore what this role might be and how teachers might respond to it.

CHAPTER

Understanding understanding in reading

Introduction

Any examination of the constituent skills of effective reading would place a high priority on the abilities of readers to understand the texts they are reading. Without understanding, readers cannot respond to, analyse or evaluate this text. Research tells us that understanding texts is not quite as straightforward as it sometimes appears, and many readers, at both primary and secondary levels, have problems with it.

The problems of understanding

To assess the problem of what to teach when teaching understanding, we must try to determine what is likely to prevent a reader from comprehending a given text. Or, to put it more positively, what must a reader know, beyond recognising the words, in order to read a text? Let us consider an actual example and use it as a guide to the problem. The example text is taken from the first two chapters of *Treasure Island*. We will take eight passages, and attempt to indicate the nature and the source of the trouble a reader might have in reading these passages.

1. Awkward expressions

> I take up my pen . . . and go back to the time when . . . the brown old seaman . . . first took up his lodging at the Admiral Benbow.

One problem readers might have in reading stories is a lack of familiarity with certain idiomatic usage, or modes of expression. Here the problem is obvious because the expression 'took up his lodging' is an out-of-date phrase. Readers may well know, or be able to figure out, what each word is, but may still be confused. They may not be able to understand what course of action the seaman is following. One aspect of learning how to track characters' actions through a story is learning to recognise the clues that indicate when a character is pursuing a given plan.

9

2. Recognising the schema

> ...took up his lodging at the Admiral Benbow.

Adult readers now realise that the Admiral Benbow is a kind of hotel (or inn, as we are later told). But how do we know that? We know it the same way we know that in 'Sam ordered a meal at The Ganges', 'The Ganges' is a restaurant, probably an Indian restaurant. We, as adult readers, recognise the scenario because we are in what is sometimes referred to as a schema. A schema is a sequence of thinking triggered by a sentence, phrase or word in the text. Some readers, however, particularly those with less experience of the world, may have difficulty in making this association. They may be unfamiliar with the 'stay at a hotel' schema. Even if they are not thrown off by the awkward phrase 'took up his lodgings', some readers will not be able to work out that the Admiral Benbow is a hotel unless they are familiar with the hotel schema.

3. Recognising plots and plans

> 'This is a handy cove,' says he at length; 'and a pleasant sittyated grog-shop. Much company, mate?'
> My father told him no, very little company, the more was the pity.
> 'Well, then,' said he, 'this is the berth for me.'

Here, in the context of the story, adult readers will recognise that the seaman is planning to stay at the inn if it is quiet and secluded enough. We assume that he is hiding, or that perhaps something even more sinister is going on and we expect to be told the reason why later. But do younger readers? In reading stories, it is important to try to determine the plans of the characters we meet. We must learn to question their motives and see the larger picture. This is a very difficult thing for a reader to learn to do. It involves a new point of view. Young readers tend to accept the people they meet at face value. They trust everybody. They do not generally see or look for sinister plans or plots. To develop expertise as a reader they must learn to ask questions like, 'What is odd about this?' and 'What if the sailor is not someone who can be trusted?'

Most, if not all, plots are based on the interaction between characters' plans as they strive to achieve their goals, the blocking of some of these plans and the success of others. Tracking such things in detail may well be beyond a young reader's experience and needs to be learnt. Watching films can help with this as it will certainly introduce viewers to complex plots and sinister plans. But there is a great difference between processing text and processing moving pictures. In reading, many more inferences must be made about what characters actually have done. In films, actions are generally spelt out in visual detail. Understanding that a character has a plan, and inferring the details of his plan, is easy when watching a film because we can watch the plan develop. We see every detail of a character's actions in front of us. In reading a story, we can assess the plot, but we must infer the details.

4. Background knowledge of characters

> And indeed bad as his clothes were and coarsely as he spoke, he had none of the appearance of a man who sailed before the mast, but seemed like a mate or skipper accustomed to be obeyed or to strike.

Would a young reader know the difference between a 'man who sailed before the mast' and 'a mate or skipper'? What comparison is being made here? Without some knowledge of what seamen of this era did, looked like, wanted, and so on, it is difficult to understand this sentence.

Two things are important here. First, if we want to help pupils understand this story, we need to give them other stories or texts which will provide them with the relevant background knowledge. Secondly, we must also teach pupils to wonder about the implications of the details of the story. They must be taught to assess the characters they meet, i.e. what kind of person is being talked about here?

5. Plot development

> He had taken me aside one day and promised me a silver fourpenny on the first of every month if I would only keep my 'weather-eye open for a seafaring man with one leg' and let him know the moment he appeared.

The plot thickens. We know that, but do the pupils? They must understand something of what a plot is, how stories develop, and so on. Again this understanding is based on tracking characters' emerging plans. Who is doing what? What does it mean? How do I know? How might I be wrong? These are questions worth reflecting upon.

6. World knowledge

> His stories were what frightened people worst of all. Dreadful stories they were – about hanging, and walking the plank, and storms at sea, and the Dry Tortugas, and wild deeds and places on the Spanish Main. By his own account he must have lived his life among some of the wickedest men that God ever allowed upon the sea, and the language in which he told these stories shocked our plain country people almost as much as the crimes that he described. My father was always saying the inn would be ruined, for people would soon cease coming there to be tyrannised over and put down, and sent shivering to their beds; but I really believe his presence did us good. People were frightened at the time, but on looking back they rather liked it; it was a fine excitement in a quiet country life, and there was even a party of the younger men who pretended to admire him, calling him a 'true sea-dog' and a 'real old salt' and such like names, and saying there was the sort of man that made England terrible at sea.

To understand this passage, you need to know something of the values and morals of an English town in the eighteenth century. Further, it is most important to know about businesses – inns in particular – and how they are run. A basic knowledge of commerce is needed here. This story can be understood effectively only in the presence of the appropriate background knowledge.

7. Recognising important objects

'Ah! Black Dog,' says he. 'HE'S a bad 'un; but there's worse that put him on. Now, if I can't get away nohow, and they tip me the black spot, mind you, it's my old sea-chest they're after.'

This line is the turning point of the story so far. It indicates that there will be a fair amount of plot associated with the sea-chest. As it turns out, what is inside the sea-chest is the crucial issue in the story. How is the young reader to know this? How do we know it? We know it because we know about valuable objects, greed, likely containers for valuable objects and story structure. When we see a particular object in a story we expect it to be used in the story. We know that, if the sea-chest were not destined to be important in this story, the author would probably not have mentioned it in the first place. Young readers may not yet have this sense of what is likely to become important and they will need to be taught to look out for significant objects and to hypothesise about the likely uses for these objects.

8. Inferences, beliefs and reasoning

I lost no time, of course, in telling my mother all that I knew, and perhaps should have told her long before, and we saw ourselves at once in a difficult and dangerous position.

Why are they in a difficult position? For adults it is obvious. Our heroes possess objects of value that others know about and will want to steal. But this is not necessarily obvious to inexperienced readers. They must be taught to construct relevant chains of reasoning based on beliefs derived from what they have heard so far, and from what they know of life. But what do readers know of life? Some of that kind of knowledge is taught by stories. Much of it must be taught when, or preferably before, a story is encountered. Readers must learn to figure out what is going on.

This analysis of the knowledge that a young reader must bring to the task of understanding a relatively short text suggests the complexity of what teachers often take for granted in readers' reading. It is often felt that, having understood the words in a text, readers can easily go on to understand the text as a whole. Understanding is, however, much more complex than this and the majority of pupils will need some teaching if they are to make the kinds of associations detailed here.

Understanding as envisionment

As they engage in reading, readers are constantly adding to and elaborating the vision of a text's meaning in their minds. Referring to this understanding as an 'envisionment' will stress the creative process involved here. Envisionments are text-worlds in the mind, and they differ from individual to individual. They are a function of one's personal and cultural experiences, one's relationship to current experience – what one knows, how one feels – and what one is trying to achieve. Envisionments are dynamic sets of related ideas, images, questions, disagreements, anticipations, arguments and hunches that fill the mind during reading. An envisionment is always either in a state of change or available for and open to change. This act of change is 'envisionment building'. Envisionment building is not just an activity occurring during reading; we build envisionments all the time when we make sense of ourselves, of others and of the world.

For example, when you meet someone for the first time – say at a party – you might have no knowledge of that person except for their physical appearance, dress, and an assumption that the individual is acquainted in some way with the person who is giving the party. With these first few clues you begin to build an envisionment of the person (more or less detailed, depending on your interest). You know that the person is a man, middle-aged (looks about 45), well-dressed, in very good taste albeit a bit formal. His reserved manner suggests that he is a private person, perhaps a bit withdrawn. He looks and sounds well-educated and professional but is somehow different from the other more academic people at the party. And so it is that you build an envisionment of who he is. At first your envisionment is filled with a few knowns, some maybes and a lot of questions. As you glean more information about this person, through conversations with and/or about him, your envisionment develops.

In reading, envisionment refers to the understanding a reader has about a text, which is also subject to change as ideas unfold and new ideas come to mind. During reading, envisionments change with time; as more of the text is read, some ideas become less important, some grow in prominence, some are added and some are reinterpreted. Even after the last word has been read and the book has been closed, the reader is left with an envisionment that is subject to change. Changes can occur through writing, additional thought, other reading or discussion. Envisionments grow and change and become enriched over time with thought and experience.

We can think of envisionment building as an activity in making sense, where meanings change and shift and grow as the mind creates its understanding of a text. There is a constant interaction (or transaction, as Rosenblatt (1978) calls it) between the person and the text, and the particular meaning that is created represents a unique meeting of the two. An envisionment is not merely visual, nor is it always a language experience. Rather, the envisionment encompasses what an individual thinks, feels and senses, sometimes knowingly, often tacitly, as she or he builds an understanding.

But what happens across time that causes our envisionments to change? As we read, we develop new thoughts. Some earlier ideas, questions and hunches no longer seem important or pertinent to our understanding; other ideas have begun to assume prominence, and to draw new questions and hunches from us. From this perspective, an envisionment represents the total understanding a reader has at any point in time, resulting from the ongoing transaction between self and text. During the reading of any particular book or play or chapter a reader has a 'local' envisionment, which changes as new thoughts (from the text, from the reader and from other people and events) lead to changes in overall understanding. In this way, a local envisionment evolves into a 'final' envisionment that is not the sum of what we thought along the way but is a modified envisionment resulting from all the changes in the local envisionments that have led to this one. Some ideas from previous envisionments remain in the final envisionment, but other parts that are no longer critical to the meaning of the text are gone. Each local envisionment is qualitatively different from the one it replaces; it is not a tree-trunk, with layers of its past within it, but rather a butterfly that is essentially unique at each new stage of life. Even after the last word is read we are left with an envisionment that is also subject to change with additional thought, reading, discussion, writing and living.

Understanding as schema building

Read the following passage which, unless you have a background in nuclear physics, you are likely to find difficult to understand. Think a bit about exactly what it is about the passage that makes it difficult to understand.

> Ilya Prigogine has demonstrated that when an 'open system', one which exchanges matter and/or energy with its environment, has reached a state of maximum entropy, its molecules are in a state of equilibrium. Spontaneously, small fluctuations can increase in amplitude, bringing the system into a 'far from equilibrium' state. Perhaps it is the instability of sub-atomic particles (events) on the microscopic level that causes fluctuations on the so-called macroscopic level of molecules. At any rate, strongly fluctuating molecules in a far-from-equilibrium state are highly unstable. Responding to internal and/or external influences, they may either degenerate into chaos or reorganise at a higher level of complexity.

You probably found it difficult to understand or remember much of this passage for the simple reason that it makes little sense to you. What is it that makes it difficult?

People commonly attribute difficulty in understanding texts to the difficult words used. This passage certainly has many obscure words which do cause difficulty. Understanding, however, relies on something a good deal deeper than just knowledge of vocabulary. To see this, read the next passage and try to make sense of it:

> The procedure is actually quite simple. First you arrange things into different groups. Of course, one pile may be sufficient depending on how much there is to do. If you have to go somewhere else due to lack of facilities that is the next step, otherwise you are pretty well set. It is important not to overdo things. That is, it is better to do too few things at once than too many. In the short run this may not seem important but complications can easily arise. A mistake can be expensive as well. At first the whole procedure will seem complicated. Soon, however, it will become just another facet of life. It is difficult to foresee any end to the necessity for this task in the immediate future, but then one can never tell. After the procedure is completed one arranges the materials into different groups again. Then they can be put into their appropriate places. Eventually they will be used once more and the whole cycle will then have to be repeated. However, that is a part of life.

In this passage there are no difficult words, yet it is still very hard to understand. However, once you are told that the passage describes the procedure for washing clothes, you can understand it perfectly easily.

What really makes the difference in understanding texts is the background knowledge of the reader. If you have adequate previous knowledge, and if you realise which particular knowledge the new passage links with, then understanding can take place. This background knowledge can be thought of in terms of structures of ideas, or schemas (Rumelhart 1985). Understanding becomes the process of fitting new information into these structures. This process is so crucial to understanding text that it is worthwhile spending a little time considering exactly how it works.

Look at the following story beginning:

The man was brought into the large white room. His eyes blinked in the bright light.

Try to picture in your mind the scene so far. Is the man sitting, lying or standing? Is he alone in the room? What sort of room is it? What might this story be going to be about?

Now read the next extract:

'Now, sit there,' said the nurse, 'and try to relax.'

Has this altered your picture of the man or of the room? What is this story going to be about?

After the first extract you may have thought the story would be set in a hospital, or perhaps concern an interrogation. There are key words in the brief beginning which trigger off these expectations. After the second extract the possibility of a dentist's surgery may enter your mind, and the interrogation scenario fades.

Each item you read sparks off an idea in your mind, each one of which has its own associated schema, or structure of underlying ideas. It is unlikely, for example, that your picture of the room, after the first extract, had a plush white carpet on the floor. You construct a great deal from very little information.

Understanding in reading is exactly like this. It is not simply a question of getting a meaning from what is on the page. When you read, you supply a good deal of the meaning to the page. The process is an interactive one, with the resultant learning being a combination of your previous ideas with new ones encountered in this text.

As another example of this, consider the following sentence:

Mary ran indoors to get her birthday money when she heard the ice-cream van coming.

Without trying too hard you can supply a great deal of information to the meaning of this, chiefly to do with Mary's intentions and feelings, but also to do with the appearance of the van and its driver's intentions. You probably do not immediately suspect him as a potential child molester. Notice that most of this seems so obvious, we barely give it much conscious thought. Our schemas for everyday events are so familiar we do not notice it when they are activated.

Now compare the picture you get from the following sentence:

Mary ran indoors to get her birthday money when she heard the bus coming.

What difference does this make to your picture of Mary, beyond the difference in her probable intentions? Most people say that she now seems rather older. Notice that this difference in understanding comes not so much from the words on the page as from the complex network of ideas to which these words make reference. These networks have been referred to as schemas, and developments in our understanding of how they operate have had a great impact upon our ideas about the nature and teaching of reading comprehension.

It appears that if new knowledge is intelligible within the schemas already existing within the mind, then it will simply be absorbed into these schemas, expanding them but not fundamentally altering their nature. This process is known as *assimilation*.

Sometimes, however, new knowledge conflicts in some way with that which is already in the mind. Then the existing schemas will need to be altered in some way to take account of the new information. This process is known as *accommodation*.

As an example of both assimilation and accommodation in action, take the case of going to a restaurant. Imagine that, while visiting a new city, I go to a restaurant that I have never been to before. How do I know how to behave, what to expect from the waiter, the order of courses I might receive, or how to order my food? I know these things from my restaurant schema which has been built up over the course of many years from all my previous experiences with restaurants. My experience in this particular restaurant simply adds to my schema, being assimilated into my existing knowledge.

Imagine, however, that my new experience is radically different from previous experiences. Suppose I have never been into a Japanese restaurant before and that this evening will mark my very first visit. The first thing I will notice is that much of my previous restaurant knowledge does not apply in this case. The restaurant certainly looks different from others I have visited; the decoration and the seating arrangements are new to me. The tables are laid very differently; the plates and cutlery are different. When it comes to the menu, this is so distinctive (even in a different script) that I will need a lot of help from the waiter to interpret it. The order of courses is different, as are my expectations of what I might drink with the meal. In a whole host of ways this experience challenges my existing restaurant schema, yet it is still distinctly a restaurant that I have entered. I need to adjust my schema quite a lot to take account of this new experience, accommodating my mind to encompass this within the new restaurant schema I take away with me.

These twin processes of assimilation and accommodation are constantly at work as readers read new material for understanding. Comprehension rests upon this active engagement of the reader with new ideas.

Conclusion

In this chapter I have attempted to explore some of the complex nature of what is usually referred to as 'reading comprehension'. Understanding text is not a simple business and, as one might expect, teaching pupils to understand it is not simple either. In the next two chapters I will look at some possible approaches to teaching pupils to comprehend both fiction and non-fiction texts.

Interactive approaches to reading fiction

Reading and re-reading: a transactional view of literacy

In her analysis of reading as a transaction, Louise Rosenblatt (1978) distinguishes between the text and the poem. By the text she means the set of marks on the page; by the poem she means the transaction that occurs as readers bring their past experience to bear on the text to create meaning. The poem, therefore, is not a thing but a process, not an object but an event. Moreover, it is a continually changing process. When a reader reads a story for the second time, his/her prior knowledge includes what is remembered from the first reading. Thus the second reading is not merely a reiteration of the first but a new process that takes its form partly from the reader's knowledge of the first reading. (N.B. When Rosenblatt uses the term 'poem', we need to understand that she is referring to the meaning created in the reader's mind as he/she interacts with the work of literature, which can be in any form – story, drama or poetry.)

A similar change occurs when readers hear or read other people's ideas about a story they have read. Because we bring our own set of experiences to the text, our individual reactions are not likely to be identical to someone else's; we each create our own 'poem' as we read the text. But hearing someone else's reactions to and ideas about that story will affect our next reading of it, whether or not we accept or value that other person's view. As an example, imagine a child reading *The Lion, the Witch and the Wardrobe* as a simple adventure story. If, during class discussion, someone compares the death of Aslan with the death of Jesus, the child may re-read the text with that idea in mind, and the second reading will be significantly affected not only by the first reading but also by the interpretation suggested during the class discussion.

Take another example. *Anne of Green Gables* tells the story of a rather wild but enchanting orphan girl who is brought up by an elderly brother (Matthew) and sister (Marilla). Students who re-read this story as part of their teacher training course usually remember how, as children, they identified with Anne. Now, as adults, they find themselves more in sympathy with Marilla. Nothing in the text has changed. The words on the page are the same as those they read ten to twenty years earlier. The changes have occurred in the reader.

What also has an impact, of course, is the reader's purpose, which affects his/her response. A child, a librarian responding to a parent's complaint about a book, a literary critic, a proofreader and the author's mother are all likely to read a text for quite different purposes – which will influence their responses to and interpretations of this text.

Implications for teaching

This transactional view of interpretation and understanding presents a serious challenge to traditional approaches to teaching, and assessing, comprehension.

One very common approach to teaching comprehension has been that of supplying readers with a text to read, and following the reading by the asking of questions, in a written or oral form. As an example of this approach, consider the following. Read the passage and try to answer the questions below it:

The chanks vos blunging frewly bedeng the brudegan. Some chanks vos unred but the other chanks vos unredder. They vos all polket and rather chiglop so they did not mekle the spuler. A few were unstametick.

Questions:

1. *What were the chanks doing?*
2. *How well did they blunge?*
3. *Where were they blunging?*
4. *In what ways were the chanks the same and in what ways were they different?*
5. *Were any chanks stametick?*

You should have found it reasonably easy to provide acceptable answers to these questions, but you will certainly feel that you do not, even now, understand this passage. What *is* a chank, and what *were* they doing?

You are able to solve language problems like this because you are a competent language user, and are able to apply your intuitive knowledge of language structures to the task. You know, for example, that the answer to a 'How well...' question will usually be an adverb (even if you do not know the actual grammatical term), and you also know that most adverbs in English end in '-ly'. If you can solve problems like this, there must be a possibility that primary children may also be able to, especially as it is reasonably well established that most children are themselves competent language users by the age of seven. This casts grave doubt on the effectiveness of comprehension exercises as a means of developing or assessing children's abilities to understand their reading. What has completing an exercise like this taught the reader? Sadly, what many children learn from experiences like this is that reading is not about interacting meaningfully with a text, but it is really about getting the questions right, which, as we have seen, they can often do without understanding.

Fortunately there are some alternative activities which can be used with children which are much more likely to involve real understanding. The transactional model of reading suggests that comprehension develops through reflection and re-reading. Consequently, useful activities will focus on one or more of two phases of reading:

■ Presentation: listening or reading.

- Reflection and re-examination: sharing impressions (drawing, talking, writing, acting, moving) and reconsidering the text.

Activities focused on phase two, arguably the most crucial of them all, should encourage the learner to return to the text. It is reflecting upon stories and re-reading them, perhaps several times, that will develop the learner's understanding. During these return visits to the text the transactions occur, and comprehension develops.

Presenting the text

Shared reading

Shared reading has become a very widely used reading activity, due to its place as one of the key activities in the literacy hour. It involves the collaborative reading of a text with a group or class and is included in this chapter because, in essence, it is an activity which begins with a meaningful text. Because the text is presented to the pupils collaboratively, the initial emphasis can be upon its meaning and their responses to it. Teaching pupils how the text works – how it is structured, how its sentences link together, how its words are constructed, and so on – can then be done within the context of this meaning.

An important part of shared reading is the demonstrations the teacher can give of how reading works in general and how to read this text in particular. Some examples of these demonstrations are:

- reading aloud with fluency and expression;
- showing the class how an experienced reader deals with difficulties in the text – what readers do, for example, if they reach a word/sentence/paragraph which they cannot understand;
- talking about the structure of the text – what the introductory paragraph does, how characters and settings are introduced and developed, how plot lines are advanced.

A key aspect to shared reading is to gradually get pupils more and more involved in the reading of the text, but always with the support of other collaborators. Such social support can help the development of confident and fluent reading and lessens the chances of pupils failing. A shared reading session might start with the teacher reading the text aloud to the group. It could also involve the group reading in unison, individuals reading short sections or the group, whose reading has been modelled for them by the teacher, re-reading a section.

There are a number of points to bear in mind when doing shared reading with a group.

(a) What kind of text to use?

A range of enlarged texts will be needed, including stories of various kinds, information texts and poetry, so that the children are able to see and hear text at the same time. These texts should have a variety of formats and lively and interesting content, and they should ideally be appropriate for extended use over three or four days in a week. Big Books are the most obvious form of text to use, but it is possible to enlarge texts in other ways. Some texts can be enlarged up to A3 size using a photocopier. It is also possible to retype some texts on a word processor and then to print out this text at 48-point size. Some technological aids can also enlarge text, such as an overhead projector.

(b) What level of difficulty should texts be?

The texts used should be within children's comprehension levels but, ideally, beyond the independent reading level of most of the class. They should, therefore, provide a challenge and be suitable for extending the children's skills.

With a mixed-age class, the difficulty levels of the texts used will need to be varied so that all children can experience an appropriate challenge on a regular basis but no children are continually at frustration level in the reading.

(c) What is the teacher's role?

The teacher needs to take a number of roles:

- to read the text with (not simply to) the class;
- to model reading behaviours such as sound–symbol correspondence and directionality;
- to teach basic concepts about print, such as book, page, word, line, letter;
- to teach and allow children to practise phonic and word recognition skills in context;
- to show children how knowledge of sentence structures and punctuation can be useful reading strategies;
- to model how understanding occurs through thinking out loud about the text as it is read;
- to show how to try to make sense of difficult words and ideas in a text;
- to help children infer unknown words from the surrounding text and to confirm these by looking carefully at their spelling patterns;
- to target teaching at a wide range of reading ability in the class by differentiating questions to stretch less able children as well as providing further reading opportunities and revision for others.

(d) What is the child's role?

The child's role is to participate in the shared reading, individually and in unison, so as to learn and practise reading skills in the context of lively and interesting texts. The key word here is 'participate'. Shared reading is not an effective teaching strategy if it simply involves a teacher reading aloud to a group. The group have to be actively involved in creating and discussing the reading.

Shared reading can be used as the starting point for a range of other work aimed at extending pupils' reading skills.

Vocabulary work

Vocabulary work will often link directly to the text used in the shared reading session. Words from that text can, for example, be used as starting points for:

- generating synonyms and antonyms – Ben's fantasy dog in *A Dog So Small* (Phillippa Pearce) was tiny. What other words do we know for 'tiny'? What words mean the opposite of tiny?

- defining words and applying them in new contexts – at the beginning of *The Hodgeheg* (Dick King-Smith) we are told that Auntie Betty has 'copped it'. What does that mean? Can you use it in another sentence? Is it an example of formal or informal language? What do we mean by 'slang'?

- exploring how writers can make up new words to express ideas that would previously have taken several words – in *Alice through the Looking Glass* (Lewis Carroll), Humpty Dumpty explains some of the words in *The Jabberwocky*, e.g. 'mome' means 'from home'; in *Little Wolf's Book of Badness* (Tony Whybrow) Little Wolf ends his letters with new ways of saying goodbye – 'Yours tiredoutly';

- investigating how new words are added to the language – in *Goodnight Mister Tom*, the word 'blitz' is used. Where does this come from?

These sessions can also create opportunities for direct teaching about the structures, organisation and purpose of vocabulary aids such as the dictionary and the thesaurus. They provide the teacher with opportunities to model the use of such aids and engage in reciprocal teaching of their use.

Punctuation work

A shared text can often provide a starting point for this work. Some examples of this include:

- noting where commas occur and discussing the way they help the reader interpret the meaning of the sentence;

- distinguishing between the use of the apostrophe to indicate possession and its use to show contraction;

- noting the setting out of speech in text, e.g. on separate lines for different speakers, and the positioning of commas before speech marks.

Grammatical awareness

The shared text can also provide a starting point for grammatical work, including, for example, getting the pupils to:

- notice the use of past tense for narration;

- compare adjectives on a scale of intensity (e.g. hot, warm, tepid, lukewarm, chilly, cold) and degree (cold, colder, coldest);

- understand the need for agreement between nouns and verbs; and

- transform sentences from active to passive and vice versa.

Guided reading

Guided reading is the other major, relatively new, teaching strategy now seen as an integral part of the literacy hour. It is, at heart, an activity that enables children, in a small-group setting, to practise being independent readers. In particular, its aim is to enable children to use a range of reading strategies in combination to problem-solve their way through a text which they have not read before and which has not yet been read to them.

Guided reading is founded on the notion that reading is a multi-strategic process and this concept underpins the approach to the teaching of reading in the literacy hour. When we read we are using a variety of clues to work out the meanings of the marks on a page (or screen). These clues are usually referred to as cue systems, or *signposts*, and include the following:

- Knowledge of individual words. Research has shown that adult readers actually recognise the majority of words they read without needing to use any other information.

- Knowledge of the letters in words and the sounds usually attached to those letters. English spelling is not as regular in its way of linking sounds to letters as many other languages, although, if we take the major units of words as syllables, or onset-rime divisions, English is more regular than if we use the phoneme as the basis.

- Knowledge of the grammatical structures possible within words and within sentences. The morphology of English makes many words decipherable even if you do not know them. If, for example, you know the word 'port', the system allows you to work out 'report', 'porter', 'reporter', 'import', 'important', etc. Knowledge of sentence grammar also helps you work out words. In, for instance, the sentence 'The teacher asked his pupils to write during a history lesson on papyrus', even if you do not know the word 'papyrus', you can work out that it must be some kind of writing surface.

- Previous knowledge of the topic of a text gives a lot of clues about the words in that text. Some specialised words are only found in particular contexts; other words have different meanings depending on the context in which they are found. You would, for example, interpret the sentence 'What is the difference between these two?' differently if it occurred in a mathematics textbook or if it occurred in an art book.

- Knowledge about the type of text that you are reading can also influence the way you read it. Nobody reads a telephone directory in the same way as they read a poem, even though there are poems that are written in a similar, list-like way.

To be a fluent reader demands the control of all these cue systems. As fluent readers read they are constantly drawing upon all these sources of knowledge. In fact, for fluent readers there is usually too much information available for reading – we tend to use only a fraction of it because we do not need all the cues available. This is the principle of redundancy in reading. There are many ways of deriving meaning from our reading but we only actually make use of a very few at once. Children, however, are not as practised or as competent at reading and need teaching to use the whole range of cues available.

Organising a guided reading session

Guided reading works best with a smallish (five or six) group of pupils who are roughly at the same stage in their reading, and with a text which they would generally be able to read on their own but which does provide some challenge and some area of difficulty that creates an opportunity for new learning. They each need a copy of the text and the teacher also needs a copy. Most picture books and chapter books can be good guided reading books. Non-scheme books can be graded, for easy management, using systems such as Individualised Reading or the Reading Recovery grades or pre-graded scheme books can be used.

The introduction to the session takes the form of a conversation between teacher and pupils about the text. The aim of this conversation is to cover the knowledge that will be needed for the pupils to be properly prepared to read the text for themselves. This knowledge will, naturally, vary according to the text and to the reading development level of the group. The following examples illustrate an introduction for children at an early stage, one for more advanced readers and one for a very advanced group.

Introducing a guided reading session for beginner readers

- Talk about the title – what do they think the story might be about?
- Relate the theme of the story to the children's own experience, e.g. if the story is about a dog, do any of the children in the group have a dog at home?
- Introduce the characters in the story, e.g. 'This is a story about two bears and their names are Big Bear and Little Bear'.
- Look through the book at the pictures discussing what seems to be going on in those pictures.
- In conversation about the book, use some phrases or words that will be helpful to children in their reading of the book, e.g. in introducing *Let's Go Home, Little Bear*, you might talk about some of the things Little Bear thinks he hears while pointing to these words on the page.

Introducing a guided reading session for a group of readers who have some independence and confidence.

A group further on in its development might need a less extensive introduction.

- Introduce the book and give them an overview, e.g. 'This story is called *Farmer Duck*. It is about a duck that has to work terribly hard on a farm because the real farmer is too lazy'.
- Use the pictures selectively, e.g. 'Let's look at what's going on in the first few pictures'.
- Give a cue to help children with an unusual phrase. 'Look at the lazy farmer, just lying there in bed. All he does is lie there and ask the duck, How goes the work? How goes the work? (N.B. Use the phrase but do not specifically point out those words on the page. If you feel you need to make the cue more explicit you might ask the children to find those words on the page.)
- Tell the children about something they will be able to find out when they read the book for themselves. 'When you read the book you'll find out how the duck makes the lazy farmer get out of bed.'

Introducing guided reading to a group of more able or experienced children

A more advanced group (e.g. a group of average Year 2 children) might need the briefest of introductions, e.g. 'This book is called *Elmer Again*. We've read a book about Elmer before. Who can remember what happened?'

After the introduction

After concluding the introduction to the text, the pupils should be asked to read it to themselves 'in a quiet voice' and to use their fingers to point to the words as they read. The teacher needs to watch the pupils as each one reads and note any hesitancy in their reading (the finger pointing will help to keep a check on this). The teacher should not intervene immediately any difficulty is encountered but should be ready to do so as soon as it is judged that a pupil needs some additional prompting.

This basic approach can be modified for readers at an early stage of development. Instead of introducing the whole book in one go the teacher might choose to guide their reading on a page-by-page basis. For example:

- giving the pupils an introduction to a page of text;
- asking them to read that page for themselves;
- giving them an introduction to the next page;
- asking them to read that page for themselves; and so on.

Finally, they can go back to the beginning and, again, independently re-read the whole book, this time in one go.

The activity can be concluded in a variety of ways by:

- discussing the text just read with the group;
- re-reading the text in unison; the purpose of this is for the teacher to model reading with expressiveness and pace; and
- setting a follow-up activity based on the guided reading text.

Guided reading with older children

With older children the focus of guided reading changes and the teacher's time and attention should be aimed not at enabling the pupils to practise independent reading, but at enabling them to analyse text – fiction and non-fiction – at a deeper level. The focus might particularly be on plot, character, setting and dialogue in fiction texts.

The purpose of guided reading at this level is to help pupils to develop more complex responses to texts, supported by references to what they have read, and to help them to take account of the views of others. The aim is to help the children:

- develop deeper and more complex responses to text;
- make inferences from subtle textual cues;
- evaluate character motivation and the author's intentions;

■ analyse the way in which authors create particular effects through their use of vocabulary, grammar, textual organisation and other stylistic devices.

In guided reading all children will need to have a copy of the same text. This might be a complete text – perhaps a short story or a poem – or it might be an extract – perhaps an excerpt from a novel. Sometimes the group might be reading the whole book over a number of weeks, one chapter at a time.

It is beneficial, in teaching literacy, to make close links between reading and writing. Through the discussion in guided reading sessions pupils can develop an explicit knowledge about text and its characteristic features, including its structures and styles. This might then lead to them writing in the particular genre for themselves.

The following example illustrates how a guided reading session with a group of Year 5/6 pupils led first to group discussion and then to individual writing tasks.

The group began by reading to themselves two extracts from *The Wizard of Oz* (Frank Baum). In the first, the heroine, Dorothy, describes the prairie country in which she lives. In the second, which occurs after the cyclone has whirled her (and her house) away to Oz, she offers a description of a quite different countryside. After they had read both extracts the teacher then discussed the following points with them:

■ How did the first part of the description make them feel? Why?

■ How did the second part of the description make them feel? Why?

■ What did the author do to create such a contrast?

Then they were given the task of rewriting both sections of the passage to reverse this contrast. This was discussed with the group for a while and several examples of possible changes were suggested. After writing their changed versions, the group then presented their work to the rest of the class during a plenary session.

Independent reading

Although shared and guided reading are extremely useful approaches to encouraging an interactive approach to understanding fiction text, there are also times when pupils should be encouraged to read independently. It seems logical to suggest that children will not become avid readers unless they are given opportunities to actually read. The same argument applies to almost any activity. Although I may learn to drive a car during a dozen or so lessons, I do not become a driver without much more opportunity to practise. For many children opportunities to engage in pleasurable reading regularly occur at home, and for these children the supportive atmosphere of a home which values books and reading is probably sufficient to ensure that they, too, will come to share these values. For others, though, school may represent the most extended opportunity to read that they get, and so it is vital that it does actually give them this opportunity.

The single factor most strongly associated with pupils' reading achievement, more than socio-economic status or any instructional approach, is the time they spend actually reading (Krashen 1993). Research has shown that the amount of leisure reading pupils do is correlated with their reading achievement. In one study (Anderson *et al.* 1983) it was found that children who were very high-achieving readers spent five times as long every day in reading books as did children who were classed as average readers. Reading promotes reading – the more pupils read the more their vocabulary grows; the more words they can read the more reading they can do.

This suggests that allowing pupils to read independently for a short time – perhaps only 15 to 20 minutes – during the school day can contribute powerfully to their language and literacy development. This activity is given a variety of names: Sustained Silent Reading (SSR), Drop Everything and Read (DEAR), Uninterrupted Sustained Silent Reading (USSR), Everyone Reading in Class (ERIC) or Sustained, Quiet, Uninterrupted, Individual Reading Time (SQUIRT). Most versions of the activity have common features:

- They often involve everyone in the class reading – including the teacher, who does not take advantage of the time to mark books, hear readers, tidy his/her desk etc., because that would indicate to the children that reading, while important, is not important enough for the teacher to do it too.

- They often occur at the beginning of school sessions, either morning or afternoon. This indicates to the children that the teacher places high importance upon them. Having them at the very end of the day might give the children the message that they were just winding-down times.

- They often involve the whole school. In some schools even the head teacher, the caretaker, school secretary and dinner ladies read at these times. This, again, indicates to the children how important these times are.

There are a number of other strategies for encouraging pupils to read independently.

Buddy reading

Buddy reading gives pupils rather less support in reading than shared or guided reading, but more than having to read completely independently. It involves pairs of pupils reading together. These may be pairs of similar ability or weaker and stronger students together. It may also involve pairs with three or more years separating their ages. The aim of the activity is for each pupil to read softly to the other, taking turns with paragraphs or pages. The job of the listening student is to help with any difficulties the reader has. After the reading, the pair discuss what they have read.

If there is a large age gap between the pupils, then an alternative way of managing buddy reading is to get pupils to use 'echo reading', that is, the older pupil reads a sentence, para-graph or page, which the younger then tries to read in exactly the same way. This can be an excellent way of encouraging both pupils to think about intonation and expression in reading.

Reader's Theatre

The Reader's Theatre activity offers a way for readers to participate in repeated readings in a meaningful and purposeful context. Rather than performing in a traditional play where the actors have costumes and props, and have to memorise their lines, in Reader's Theatre pupils read aloud from a script using their voices and facial expressions to share the story. This format provides an opportunity for pupils to develop fluency in reading through multiple readings of a text, using expressiveness, intonation and inflection.

Reader's Theatre scripts can be written by teachers themselves, based on a story they may have already read to a class. There are also plenty of scripts freely available for teachers to download from the internet: American children's author Aaron Shepherd, for example, has a website devoted to Reader's Theatre where he supplies lots of scripts suitable for pupils aged 8 to 15 (www.aaronshep.com/rt/index.html). A collection of scripts for younger pupils, including lots of choral poems, can be found at the Reader's Theatre website (http://www.readerstheatre.ecsd.net/collection.htm).

Using audio-taped books

Tape-recorded books can be a valuable tool for motivating readers, giving them supported reading practice, and at the same time providing a model of good reading. Pupils can listen to a story on cassette while following along in their copies of the book. While listening to the story over and over again they learn to associate the spoken word with the printed word. Not only does listening to tapes enrich vocabulary and word recognition but it also provides the listener with reading that is fluent, accurate and expressive. Listening and following along in the book focuses on interpretation and allows the reader/listener to become involved in the story.

A number of research studies have found positive effects from the sustained use of audio-taped books. Carbo (1978) reports her work with slower readers in which she found that the use of audio-taped books, as long as they contained readings at a slow enough rate, did enhance the abilities of readers to engage with the texts they were using. Topping and his colleagues (1997) found that the use of audio-taped books significantly enhanced the reading skills and motivation towards reading of a range of primary school pupils, a result confirmed by Byrom's (1997) smaller-scale, but more detailed, work.

Many teachers have invested in listening centres for their classrooms where groups of up to six pupils can listen to the same recorded story while following the text in a copy of the book.

Reflecting on the text

There are a wide range of activities which encourage readers to reflect upon the text they have just read (or had read to them). In the following section I will describe several of these activities, but it is important to stress at this point that these are not merely a 'smorgasbord' of activities to be used indiscriminately. Each activity should only be used if it is appropriate for a particular group of pupils and a specific text.

If each of the activities that follow is to be used effectively, it is also important for teachers to understand the transactional nature of reading, as discussed earlier. The implication of this is that there will rarely be a 'correct' answer in the following activities (although there will be incorrect ones). The key intention is to get pupils to reflect upon what they have read and make sense of it in their own terms and in collaboration with others. All these activities should involve a great deal of discussion, and it is with talking about books that we should begin.

Book talk

Aidan Chambers (1993) has written powerfully about the importance of talk about books and the 'reading conference' has become an established part of teaching practice in American and Australian schools. Talking about books, with other pupils or with adults, gives readers the opportunity to test out their ideas about the meanings of a story and also to develop these ideas as they encounter those of others.

In some classrooms, groups of pupils regularly meet in 'literature circles' to discuss their reactions to the stories they have read or had read to them. Literature circles work best when there is no written outcome – if the point of the circle is to produce a piece of work then that is what pupils will focus on, rather than exploring tentative ideas about a story. This is not to say that the group cannot be asked to focus upon specific things in their circle meeting; it can be very useful to ask them to discuss questions such as:

- Who was your favourite character in the story, and why?
- Did the story end as you thought it would? How else might it have ended? (Questions like this will begin to develop pupils' critical literacy – see Chapter 8.)
- Was the setting important in this story, or could it have been set anywhere else?
- Did the story make you feel happy/sad/relieved?
- What other stories have you read by this author? Did you like them as much, more or less than this one?

Although written outcomes will generally not help to get the best out of pupils during literature circle work, there are, of course, many activities in which they do have a place.

Collaborative stories

In this activity pupils are asked to create their own stories in response to a version of a picture book which has had the text removed. This requires collaboration between the original and the new (pupil) author. The strength of this activity is that it gives readers the opportunity to create meaning at the text level. In doing this they become more aware of story structure and character development, rather than just sentence and word meaning. It also has the advantage that it can be used to introduce pupils to texts well beyond their usual reading levels.

The activity needs a no-text version of a picture book. These can be created in a number of ways:

- real picture books can have their text covered with tippex or white masking tape;
- post-its or strips of paper can be placed over the text; and
- the text can be covered, and pages can be photocopied or scanned into a computer, then printed (the latter has the advantage that, with a colour printer, illustrations can retain their colour).

The teacher first shares the original story with an individual, group or class. With less skilful readers, the teacher can read it to them, whereas more proficient readers might read it themselves. Once the text has been read (not necessarily the same day), the pupils are ready to produce their own versions. They may decide to reproduce a similar story using their own language (without looking back at the text), or to try to produce a completely different version of the story. When this has been done, they then share the new text with other readers. Some might then like to go back to the original text to see how the new text is different.

A useful variation of this activity is to use the pictures from a story which the pupils have not seen before. Although this changes the nature of the lesson, they still have to use a similar knowledge of language to construct the text. What this variation offers is complete freedom from the constraints of the original text stored in pupils' memories.

Text sequencing

This involves cutting up a text into pieces (using logical divisions based on meaning) and presenting the text segments to small groups of four to six pupils. As with the previous activity, it requires the reader to create meaning at the text level. In particular, pupils need to use their knowledge of story structures.

To use this activity a text of 200–500 words is ideal. It is better if the text is typed or scanned as this enables it to be reformatted so that pupils do not simply rely on clues such as the section beginning with a sequence of words which physically fit the gap left at the end of the previous section. The focus of the pupils should be on meaning and text structure rather than physical clues. It is useful to glue the segments of text onto pieces of cardboard of uniform size and to then distribute these among the group. The group is then asked to try to reconstruct the text. At first the teacher might need to help them by asking questions such as 'Who thinks they have the first part?' and 'Why do you think that piece comes next?' However, it does not take long for most pupils to learn how to negotiate the activity without assistance.

As a variation to this activity, it can be useful to provide the group with one or two blank cards (deliberately leaving out sections of the text). The group must also place the blank cards in position and write the missing text segments themselves.

Story retelling

The essential purpose of this activity is to get pupils to reconstruct a text that will then be shared with a larger audience. The text may have been read to the group by the teacher or it could have been read independently. Following the reading of the story, the pupils are asked to provide a verbal retelling of the story, with props to support their presentation. For example, they might use silhouettes on an overhead projector, a time-line, dramatisation, mime, puppetry, etc. By encouraging them to experiment with other methods of making meaning, they are then able to share the meaning they have created with other pupils.

Character profiles

Character profiles are a simple device to focus readers' attention upon the personalities of specific characters in a text. Their use encourages pupils to consider not only the personality traits of the character but also the relationships between different characters. Although the composition of the character profile sheet can vary, the format shown in Figure 3.1 is particularly useful.

Name of character:
Picture:
Age:
Description:
Special features:
What was he or she trying to do in the story?

FIGURE 3.1 A character profile outline

One way of using character profile sheets is for the teacher to first demonstrate filling one in, using a character that all the pupils are familiar with, preferably one from a piece of literature they have recently read. Pupils then compile their own profile of a different character from the current class story, working either individually or in small groups. They can then be given the opportunity to share these with other members of the class. This is not only extremely enjoyable, but it also gives them a chance to hear how others have represented the same, or a different, character from the same book.

The profile sheet can obviously be changed simply by adding or deleting specific categories of information. For example, they might add categories like 'favourite TV programme', 'how he/she spends his/her spare time', 'last seen', and so on. The profile could also be changed into a 'Wanted' poster, and then displayed around the room.

Never-ending story

This activity integrates reading and writing. Pupils are provided with the beginning of a story which they must continue to write, until they are told to pass the story on to another pupil for it to be continued. The activity requires reading and writing in an interactive way: first reading, then writing, reading, then writing, and so on. It also requires the reader/writer to construct meaning for extended texts (both through reading and writing). Each time a new text is passed on to the next pupil it is necessary for him or her to read the text that has already been written, predict what the author was trying to create and plan how to extend the text. In a sense, this activity forces the reader to 'read like a writer' in a way that is difficult to achieve simply through conventional writing lessons.

It is useful to introduce this activity by modelling it on an overhead projector. After displaying the beginning of the story (selected from any piece of literature), the teacher then writes the next section of the text. After writing several sentences he/she stops, reads the text out aloud and asks the group to suggest what might come next. Someone's suggestion is then written as the next section of the text. The activity continues in this way until the text is completed to the group's satisfaction.

When pupils do this activity, it should be explained that they will only be given a limited amount of time to write something, and that they will then have to pass it on to another writer. Ideally, the activity should be used with groups of four to eight children. The story's beginning should only be two or three sentences long. It should introduce a character, set a little of the scene and perhaps even provide some initiating event. Each pupil in the group receives a copy of the story's beginning and is then asked to start writing. After about three minutes they pass the text on. Once each piece has been finished it is returned to the person who started it and it is then shared with the whole group.

Story maps

Story maps are graphic organisers that can be useful in helping a reader analyse or write a story. They focus on the elements of the story including the important characters (their appearance, personality traits and motivations), the setting of the story (time and place), the problem faced by the characters, how the problem is approached, and the outcome.

There are many types of story maps that examine different elements of the story:

- some simply summarise the beginning, middle and end of a story (see Figure 3.2);
- some focus on the setting, characters, problem, event and resolution of the story (see Figure 3.3 for a blank story map like this and Figure 3.4 for a map completed after a group read *A Treeful of Pigs* by Arnold Lobel);
- some list the 5 Ws: the Who, When, Where, What and Why of a story (see Figure 3.5 for a chart version of this type of story map and Figure 3.6 for an alternative version); and
- some, like a storyboard, are pictorial and illustrate the major events of a story in chronological order.

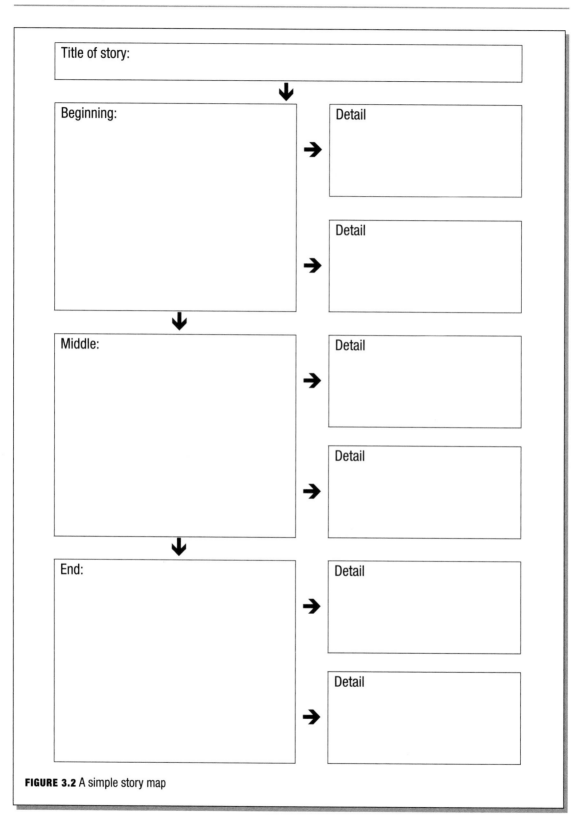

FIGURE 3.2 A simple story map

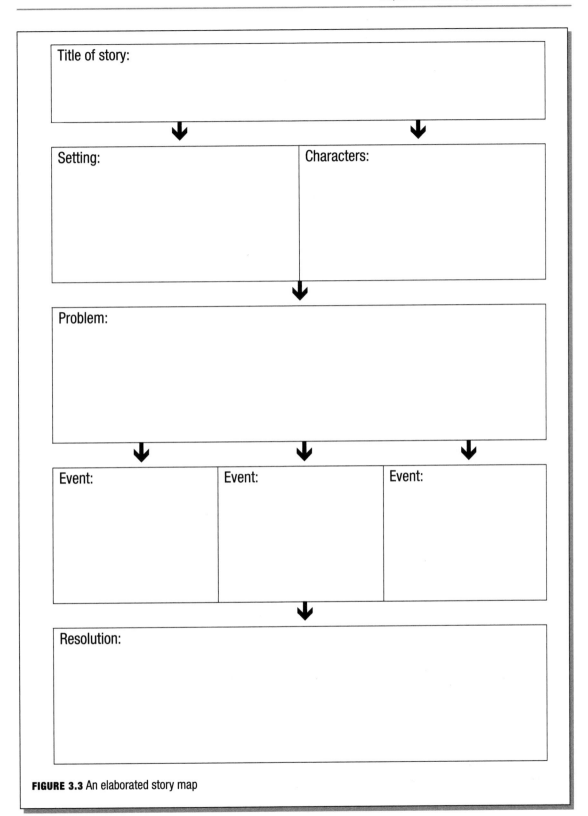

FIGURE 3.3 An elaborated story map

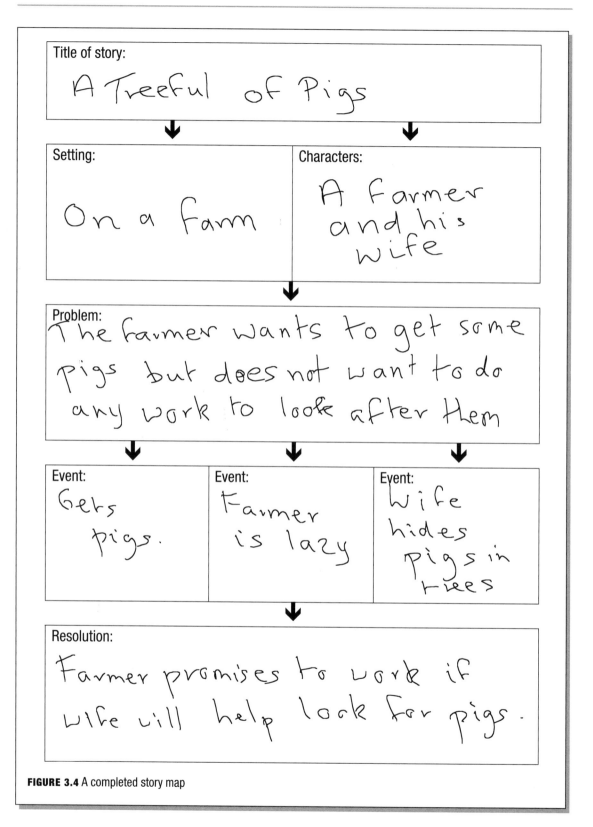

Title of story:

A Treeful of Pigs

Setting:

On a farm

Characters:

A farmer and his wife

Problem:

The farmer wants to get some pigs but does not want to do any work to look after them

Event:

Gets pigs.

Event:

Farmer is lazy

Event:

Wife hides pigs in trees

Resolution:

Farmer promises to work if wife will help look for pigs.

FIGURE 3.4 A completed story map

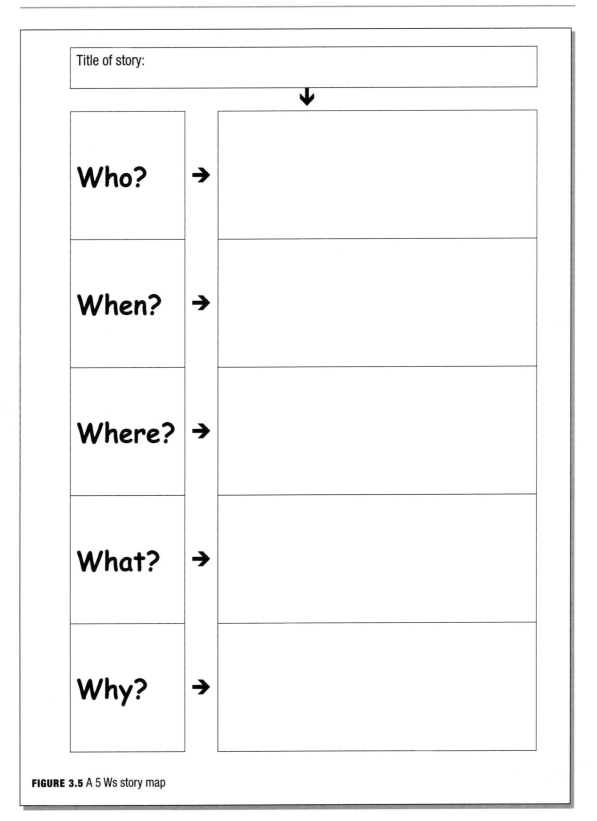

FIGURE 3.5 A 5 Ws story map

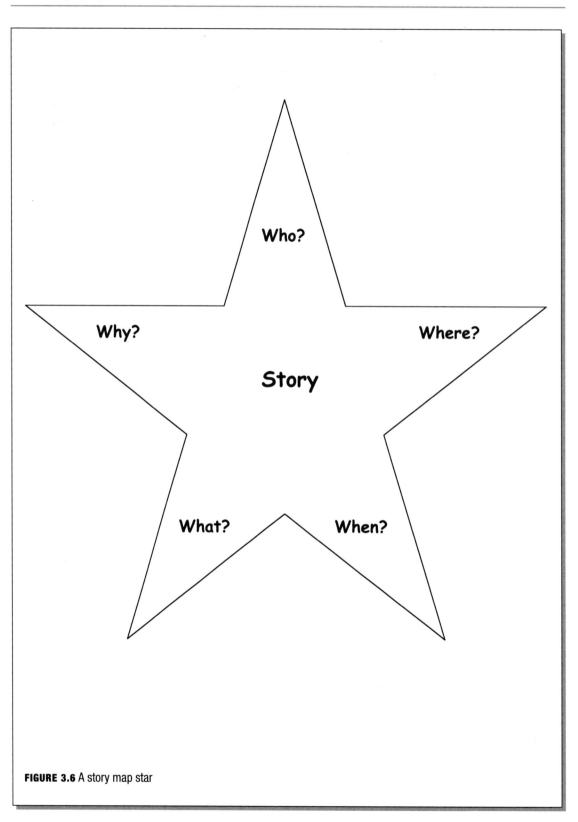

FIGURE 3.6 A story map star

Conclusion

The strategies outlined in this chapter show that there is an alternative to traditional comprehension exercises. Although these activities are all different they share many common features:

- they help readers to create meaning as they encounter texts;
- they require readers to construct a coherent understanding of whole texts;
- they encourage the use of other forms of meaning-making (such as writing, drawing, dramatisation etc.) to create a more complete understanding of the text that is read; and
- the teacher is vitally involved as a facilitator, modelling and demonstrating strategies that effective readers use to make sense of texts.

These ideas are not meant to be exhaustive; rather they are meant to act as examples of the types of strategies that can be planned for literary texts. The way teachers use the above ideas, and the alternative strategies that teachers themselves develop, will vary depending upon the text being read, the pupils being taught and the context within which the lesson takes place. It is important that this should be so. The ideas outlined must never become activities that are ends in themselves. The focus must always be upon the book or story, not the strategies that the teacher is using to help the pupils get inside the book.

Interactive approaches to non-fiction reading

Finding out

Zoe is a ten-year-old with reading difficulties. Her class is currently studying 'Living things' as their topic in science. For this lesson Zoe and her group have been asked to choose a particular living thing which interests them and to 'find out about it'. Zoe and her friends have chosen dolphins and have picked out several information books from their class collection. For the next 45 minutes or so they work quietly and diligently with these books.

Towards the end of the lesson Zoe's support teacher arrives and goes to check on what the girls have done. In Zoe's book she finds the piece of writing shown in Figure 4.1.

Most teachers will recognise what has happened here. Zoe has copied, word for word, from one or more information books. She asks Zoe to read out what she has written but Zoe finds this nearly impossible to do. She also asks Zoe what she thinks she has learnt about dolphins, but Zoe cannot really think of much. She has not processed what she has written beyond simply recognising that it is about dolphins. She has learnt very little from the lesson.

Research (e.g. Wray and Lewis 1992) suggests that most primary children know quite well that they should not copy directly from information books. Many children can give good reasons for this. Eight-year-old Anna, for example, claimed that 'you learn a lot more if you write it in your own words'. Yet, when faced with the activity of finding out from books, most children, at some stage, resort to copying. Why is this so common and how can teachers help children read for information more effectively?

The task and the text

One important part of the problem seems to be the nature of the task children are often given when using information books. Zoe's task of 'finding out about' a topic is a common one but one which is not very helpful in focusing her on understanding what she finds. If the task is to find out about dolphins, then presumably any information about dolphins is acceptable. As Zoe discovers, there are whole books full of information about dolphins. How can she choose among all this information? She has no way of narrowing down the task and it becomes unmanageable. She really needs help, before looking in the books, in deciding what she wants to find out about dolphins.

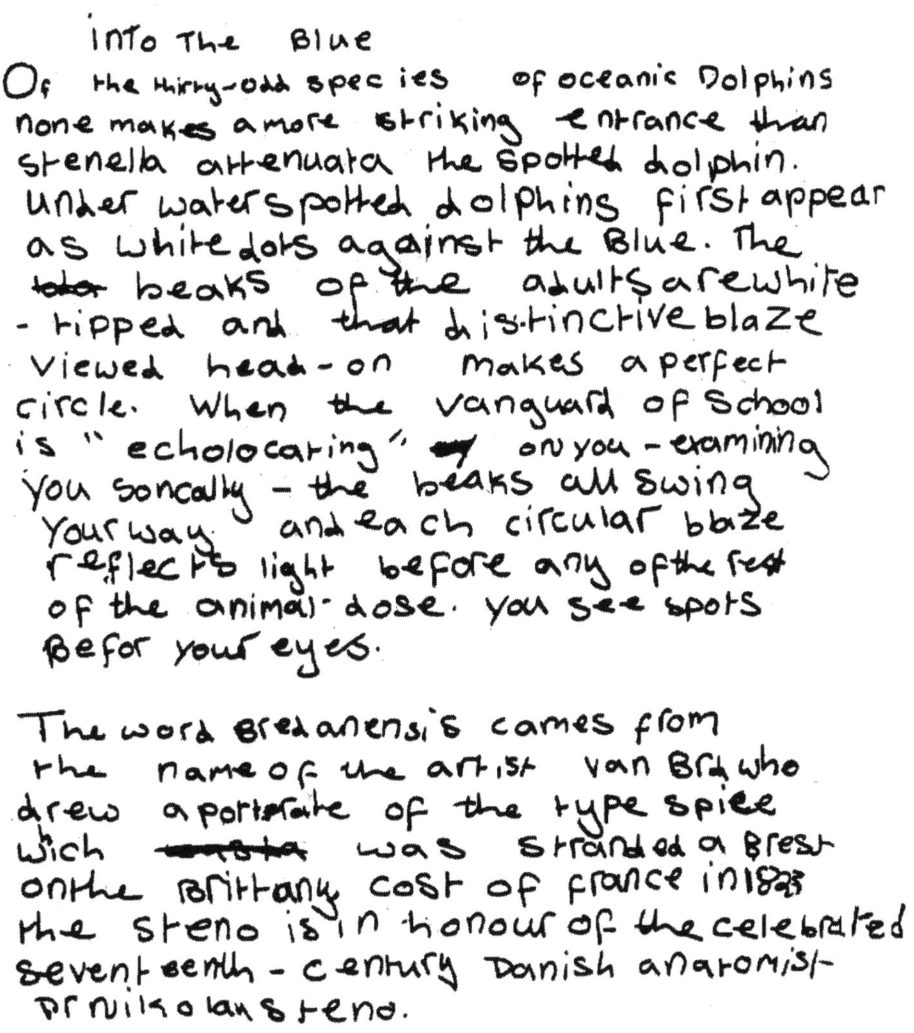

> Into The Blue
>
> Of the thirty-odd species of oceanic Dolphins none makes a more striking entrance than stenella attenuata the spotted dolphin. Under water spotted dolphins first appear as white dots against the Blue. The beaks of the adults are white - tipped and that distinctive blaze viewed head-on makes a perfect circle. When the vanguard of school is "echolocating" on you - examining you soncally - the beaks all swing your way and each circular blaze reflects light before any of the rest of the animal dose. you see spots before your eyes.
>
> The word Bredanensis cames from the name of the artist van Bra who drew a portrate of the type spiee wich was stranded a Brest on the Brittany cost of france in 1823 the steno is in honour of the celebrated seventeenth - century Danish anatomist Dr nilsolans teno.

FIGURE 4.1 Zoe's initial writing

Even if children manage to use 'information retrieval skills' well enough to locate material on the required topic, they still often find the text in that material difficult to deal with. Children in primary classrooms tend to lack experience of the different genres of non-fiction and their organisational structures (Littlefair 1991). They find the linguistic features (vocabulary, connectives, cohesion, register) more difficult to comprehend than those of the more familiar narrative texts. Most children need support from teachers to enable them to cope more easily with the problems of factual text. There are a number of teaching strategies which can provide this support and make the activity of reading information a much more purposeful one.

What do I know and what do I want to know?

Zoe's support teacher did not leave things as they were. She was due to spend a lesson working with Zoe, so she decided to introduce a different way of approaching the task. At the end of the lesson Zoe had produced a very different piece of writing about dolphins (see Figure 4.2).

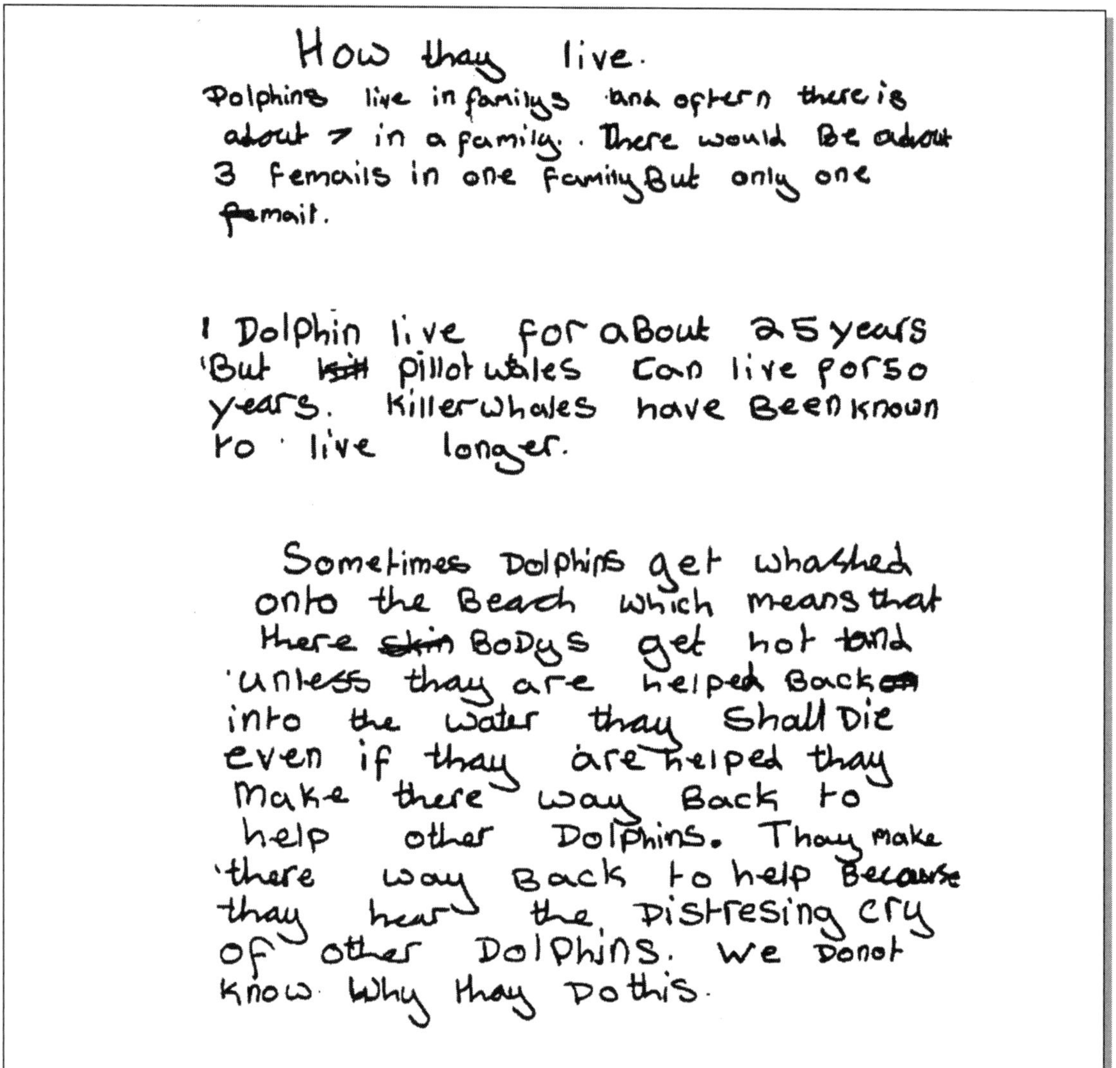

> ### How thay live.
>
> Dolphins live in familys and oftern there is about 7 in a family. There would Be about 3 femails in one Family But only one femail.
>
> 1 Dolphin live for aBout 25 years But pillot wales can live por 50 years. Killer whales have Been known to live longer.
>
> Sometimes Dolphins get whashed onto the Beach which means that there BoDys get hot and unless thay are helped Back into the water thay Shall Die even if thay are helped thay make there way Back to help other Dolphins. Thay make there way Back to help Because thay hear the Distresing cry of other Dolphins. We Donot know why thay Do this.

FIGURE 4.2 Zoe's final writing

How had the support teacher moved Zoe on from passive copying to what appears to be a more thoughtful extension of her understanding about this topic? The first step was to close the information books Zoe had been using. In teaching pupils to read non-fiction texts for understanding, an important part of the process occurs *before* the eyes meet the page. The teacher asked Zoe to think about two of the most crucial questions in any experience of reading for information:

- What do I already know about this topic?
- What do I want to know about it?

The importance of the first of these questions should be clear from the previous chapter. As we saw then, understanding is built upon the schemas already in the learner's mind. But we carry around a multitude of schemas. When we read it is necessary that the appropriate schemas are triggered before we approach the texts. For accomplished readers this can be an automatic process – we see the title of a text and it immediately brings into our minds information we already know that will help us in subsequent understanding. Less expert readers might need a bit of help in this triggering, and their teachers can actively help them activate relevant previous knowledge.

Many teachers already use discussion to activate previous knowledge but there are a range of other approaches to this which have the added advantage of giving the teacher some record of what children seem to know about a particular topic. One especially useful device is the KWL grid. This is a simple but effective strategy which both takes children through the steps of the research process and also records their learning. A KWL grid consists of three columns (see Figure 4.3).

What do I KNOW about this topic?	What do I WANT to know about this topic?	What have I LEARNT about this topic?

FIGURE 4.3 A KWL grid

Teaching Literacy

Zoe's support teacher introduced her to the strategy by drawing a KWL as three columns in Zoe's book. She then asked Zoe what she already knew about dolphins and acted as a scribe to record Zoe's responses. What Zoe knew can be seen in the first column of Figure 4.4. In the introductory stages of teaching the strategy, as for most new strategies and skills, teacher modelling is very important. Only when the child is thoroughly familiar with the strategy should they be encouraged to attempt it independently.

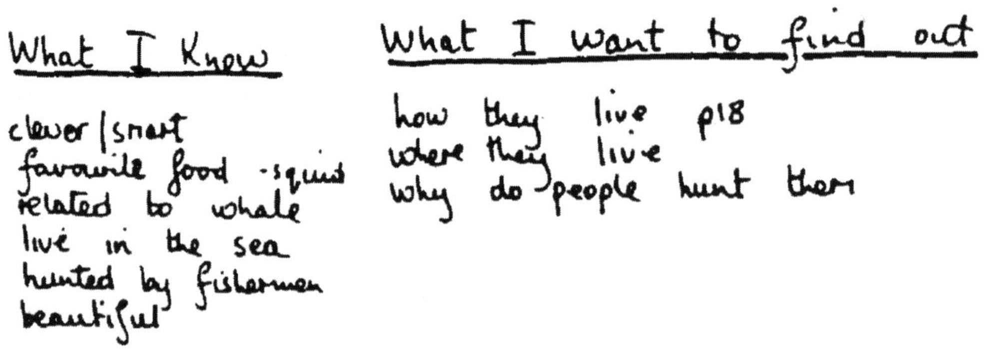

FIGURE 4.4 Zoe's KWL grid

Not only did this tapping into previous knowledge have a vital role to play in helping Zoe comprehend the texts she was to read, it also gave her an active role in the topic right from the beginning. By asking her what she knew her self-esteem and sense of 'ownership' of knowledge were enhanced, rather than being faced instantly with the (for her) negative experience of tackling a text without knowing quite how she was to make sense of it.

The next stage was to help Zoe establish some purposes for her reading by asking her what she wanted to know now. This was aimed at helping to focus her subsequent reading. What Zoe had originally been asked to do ('find out about dolphins'), although a very common way of approaching this kind of task, is actually far too broad to be useful. How could Zoe answer this? There are books full of information about dolphins so she could perhaps be forgiven for thinking that the real purpose of the task she had been set was to accumulate as much information as she could, rather than understand what she read.

This time, the discussion and the recording of what she already knew was enough to generate further questions for Zoe, questions which she would be interested in researching. These were again scribed by the teacher (see the second column of Figure 4.4).

In this case Zoe generated her own questions, but when children find this difficult there are a number of question-setting strategies that can be use with them:

■ turning what I know statements into questions, e.g. 'Whales are hunted by fishermen' can become, 'Why are whales hunted by fishermen?';

42

- introducing them to the six question words, i.e. what, where, when, why, who, how?; and
- using various graphic forms to add child appeal, e.g. question trees, question hands and question wheels with questions on each branch, finger and spoke.

On this occasion Zoe and her teacher decided to concentrate on just one question (they had only an hour together) and she was encouraged to brainstorm around her 'How do they live?' question. Again her teacher scribed and the resultant concept map can be seen in Figure 4.5.

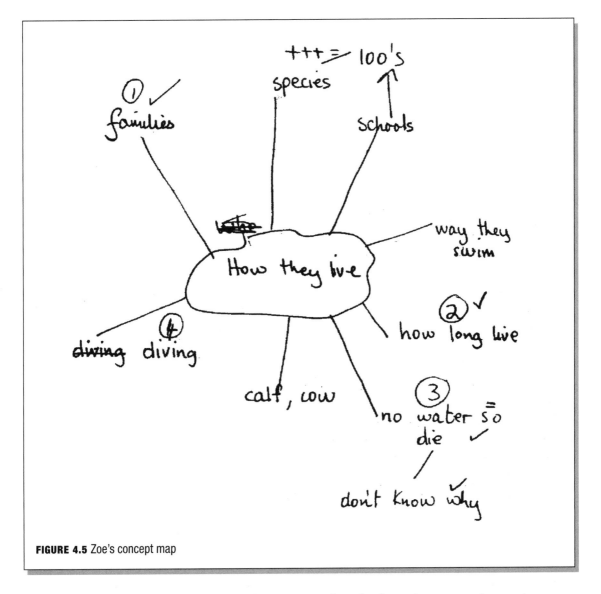

FIGURE 4.5 Zoe's concept map

The sub-questions generated by this were numbered to keep the process clear and manage-able and at this point Zoe was ready to return to her information books to try to find the answers to her questions. Now Zoe also had key words which she could use to search the index/contents etc. Sometimes her teacher wrote the word on a piece of card for her so that she could run it down the index/page and match the word. This gave her practice in scanning. We can see from the writing she had completed by the end of the session (Figure 4.2) that she was working her way logically through the questions (she had completed 1 and 2) and not only had she learnt something about dolphins but she had also had a powerful lesson on how to set about reading for information.

Other strategies

Grids such as the KWL can not only provide a written record of children's approaches to the activity of reading for information but the format of the grid also acts as an organiser, helping children see more clearly the stages of their research. It gives children a logical structure for tackling research tasks in many areas of the curriculum and it is this combination of a simple but logical support scaffolding that seems to be so useful to children.

Of course, when children are asked what they know about something, there is no guarantee that what they say they know will in fact be true. Figure 4.6, for example, shows the KWL grid completed by two Year 3 girls working collaboratively to record what they already knew about the Vikings. Notice how this gives the teacher access to some misconceptions ('They live in straw houses', for example). These can become the focus for research undertaken by the children who can then play an active role in correcting such misconceptions.

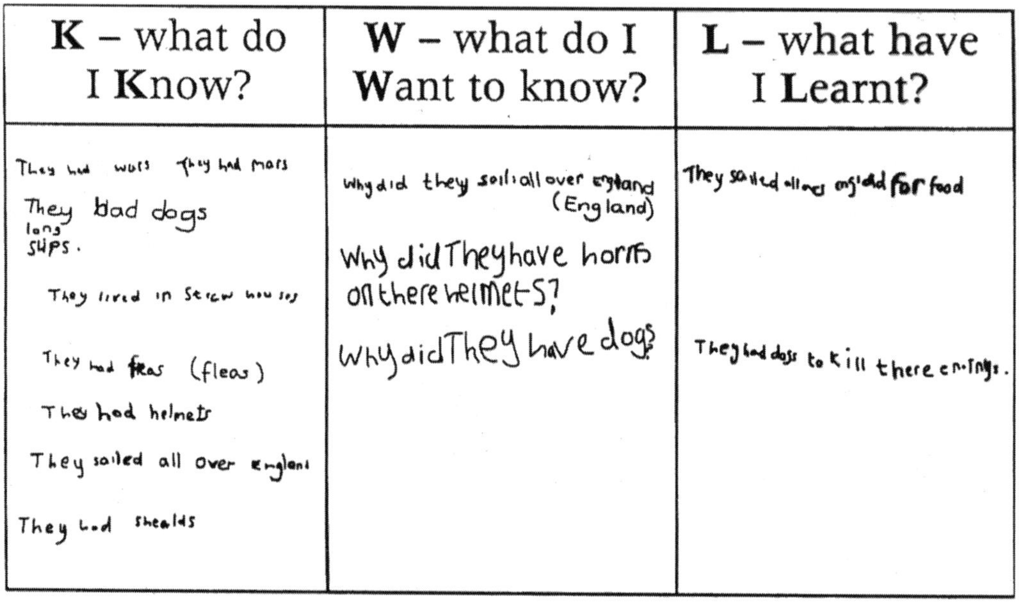

K – what do I Know?	W – what do I Want to know?	L – what have I Learnt?
They had wors they had mars They had dogs long slips. They lived in straw houses They had fleas (fleas) They had helmets They sailed all over england They had shealds	Why did they soil all over england (England) Why did They have horns on there helmets? Why did They have dogs?	They sailed along onsidd for food They had dogs to kill there enemys.

FIGURE 4.6 A KWL about the Vikings

The grid can also be extended by the addition of a fourth column so it becomes a KWFL, the F standing for 'Where will I FIND the information?' An example of this can be seen in Figure 4.7 which records some of the research of a Year 5 class into Kenya.

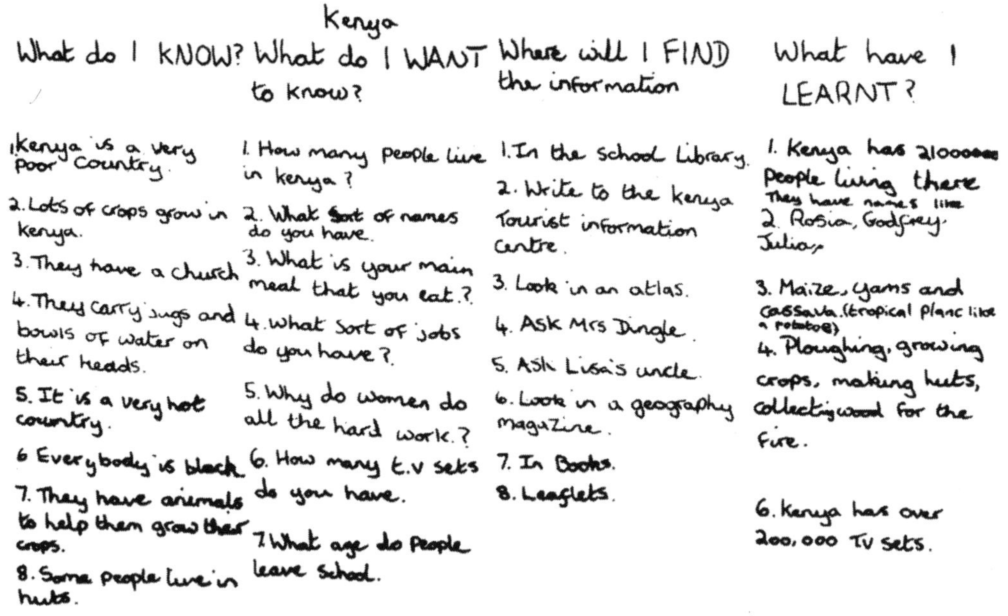

Kenya

What do I KNOW?	What do I WANT to know?	Where will I FIND the information	What have I LEARNT?
1 Kenya is a very poor country.	1. How many people live in kenya?	1. In the school Library.	1. Kenya has 2100000 people living there
2. Lots of crops grow in kenya.	2. What sort of names do you have.	2. Write to the kenya Tourist information Centre.	They have names like 2. Rosia, Godfrey. Julia,
3. They have a church	3. What is your main meal that you eat.?	3. Look in an atlas.	3. Maize, yams and cassava (tropical planc like a potatoe)
4. They carry jugs and bowls of water on their heads.	4. what sort of jobs do you have?	4. Ask Mrs Dingle.	4. Ploughing, growing crops, making huts, collectiywood for the Fire.
5. It is a very hot country.	5. Why do women do all the hard work.?	5. Ask Lisa's uncle.	
6 Everybody is black.	6. How many t.v sets do you have.	6. Look in a geography magazine.	6. Kenya has over 200,000 Tv sets.
7. They have animals to help them grow their crops.	7 What age do People leave School.	7. In Books.	
8. Some people live in huts.		8. Leaflets.	

FIGURE 4.7 A KWFL about Kenya

The grid shows that the children realise that there are more sources of useful information than merely information books, and asking them to list some of these sources has prompted their thinking about information.

Another useful grid is the QUADS grid which consists of four columns – Questions, Answer, Details, Source – and again provides a simple framework for recording information, including the child's questions. Figure 4.8 shows the QUADS grid of a seven-year-old who has raised a wide range of questions in his research into the diplodocus. The class had initially shared all they knew about dinosaurs before each child selected a dinosaur that was to feature in a story they were to write.

An interesting feature of the QUADS grid is the splitting of the answer into answer/details. This can be discussed with children in terms of the 'short' answer and the 'long' answer. By asking children to think about any information they may have discovered in these terms they are asked to summarise first and then give details. This begins to introduce the idea of making a brief note of the key information and is a very useful strategy to guide children away from merely copying down a chunk of information. Look, for example, at Lee's answer to 'What did they eat?' or 'How big were they?' and see how he has obviously reordered the information he read in the information book he was using.

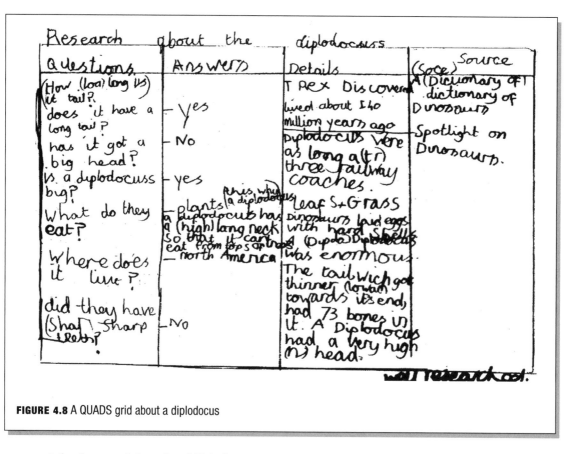

FIGURE 4.8 A QUADS grid about a diplodocus

A further useful study skill habit is encouraged by the inclusion of the Source column. Children are encouraged to note where they found the information in case they need to recheck or need to share it with another. Lee, at seven, and at his first attempt, has not recorded his source fully. He may find it useful to note details such as page numbers and authors of books, for example, but given discussion with and support from his teacher, and further opportunities to note down his sources, he will undoubtedly refine the skill. He is clearly already beginning to develop his skill at being a researcher.

Finding the answers

Locating information is often thought of as central to the process of reading for information effectively. It is arguable, however, that, although necessary, this is a minor and relatively easy part of the information-using process. Locating information includes that part of the process which involves pupils in making decisions about where they might find the required information and then in using specific study skills, such as using an index or searching a database, in order to locate the details they need. The problems with this stage of the process lie not with the complexity of the skills involved but in the children's readiness to select and use the appropriate strategy that would enable them to achieve their purpose most effectively. There is evidence (Wray and Lewis 1992) that children may know how to use an index, consult a library catalogue and use a CD-ROM, but that, when engaged on an information-finding task, they often fail to operate such strategies. Instead, they may browse through a book, randomly search a shelf of books, ask a friend and so on. It is possible that the mismatch between what pupils 'know' in their heads and what they actually do when confronted by a real task may well be caused by the way in which these skills are taught to children.

It is very common to find, in classrooms and in publisher's catalogues, books of exercises or worksheets that claim to teach 'study skills'. These often consist of exercises to give children practice in skills such as using an index. They are given an example of an index and then asked several questions which require them to use this. After completing several such worksheets children should, it is claimed, now be able to use index pages and the same process will also hold good for other devices such as contents pages. Most teachers will, however, have had lots of experience to contradict this claim. The reality is that pupils are often skilled at completing such worksheets but fail to transfer the skill to use with real books.

There are several ways to teach information finding in more contextualised ways.

Using non-fiction 'big books'

Key Stage 1 teachers are usually very aware of the advantages of using enlarged versions of fiction texts, offering as they do the opportunity for groups of children to be able to see the text clearly, and providing the teacher with a vehicle to model how to use the features of that particular book and how to read it appropriately. The same approach can be taken with non-fiction books, which provide a useful aid for teachers to model appropriate information-finding strategies and demonstrate a quick skim-read, scanning for a specific item of information/name and so on.

Using big books, or working with a group as they undertake a research task, the teacher can demonstrate what it is you actually do – not by merely telling but by showing, and accompanying the showing with a monologue of her thought processes. For example, one group of children had asked 'How long does a chick stay a chick?' Using the big book version of *The Life of a Duck* (Magic Beans series, Heinemann, 1989) the teacher modelled for the group how they might use an information book to answer the question, but as she did so she talked about what she was doing and why. She made what is usually an internal monologue accessible to the children. The conversation went something like:

> Now, Joanne asked about ducklings growing into ducks. How can I see if this book has anything on ducklings? What shall I do? Shall I read it from the beginning? No, that would take too long. I could look in the index. This list of words at the back, that tells me what's in the book. Yes, I can look in the index. Let's look up ducklings in the index. So I'm going to turn to the back of the book. Here it is. Index. Now…It's arranged alphabetically a, b, c, so d should be next…here it is, D. Can anybody see the word duckling in this column?…

This kind of modelling – making explicit to the children the thought processes she is going through as she is experiencing them – gives the children some very important lessons on what it is an experienced reader does. The teacher's explicit vocalisation of the activity provides the children with a 'learning script' which they can 'parrot' when they are trying the task. For younger and/or inexperienced learners, the script often remains explicit. All teachers will have observed young children talking themselves through a task, but as they become more skilled the script becomes internalised and, finally, operates almost unconsciously, only being called to the surface again in tricky situations.

Simple support strategies

Extra support strategies can be used by less-skilled readers or younger children in the early stages of learning to use an index and contents. Children can be encouraged to write the word they are looking for on a piece of card, underlining the first letter. Turning to the index they can then match the first letter with the appropriate alphabetical section before running the card down the section until they match the word. The page numbers can then be copied from the index onto the card. This helps the child recall which pages they need to visit (they can cross out the numbers as they do so) thus helping them hold that stage of the process in their mind without having to constantly turn back to the index. Having turned to the page the children can be helped to scan for the word by running the card quickly over the print, looking to match the word they have written. Having located the word the children can then read the sentences immediately before and after the name to see if they contain the desired information.

Interacting with information text

Reading the text on the page is obviously at the heart of the process of reading for information. There are a variety of strategies for helping children engage more productively with this text.

Text marking

Text-marking techniques, such as underlining, are used by many adults when they wish to note something in a text as being of significance. Of course, we cannot encourage children to write on school books but we can use text marking on teacher-prepared information sheets or on photocopies of pages from books. We need to use the strategy in a focused way with children. This can involve, for example, using different colours to mark information in response to particular questions.

Children might also be asked to underline the sentence they think contains the main idea of a text. Different children may choose to underline different sentences and this can be used as a discussion point when children share and justify their decisions. They can also be asked to underline the most important sentence in each paragraph. Putting these sentences together should give them an outline summary of the whole passage.

Text can also be numbered to identify sequences of events. This is especially useful where steps in a process being described are separated by chunks of texts and children might lose the thread of the basic events.

Text restructuring

The essence of this strategy is to encourage children to read information and then show the information in some other way. In doing so they have to 'pass the information through their brain' – that is, work at understanding it. Restructuring thus also gives teachers access to children's levels of understanding and can be a useful assessment strategy.

There are many different ways to restructure text. Figure 4.9 shows the work produced by a group of Year 5 children who had read a text about the process of mummification in Ancient Egypt. They marked the text to show the stages of the process and then drew a series of pictures to represent these stages. The next day, and without further access to the original text, they wrote captions to accompany their pictures.

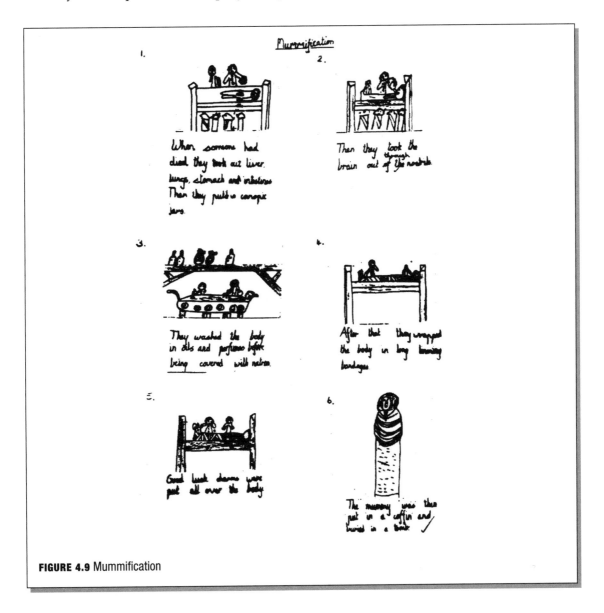

FIGURE 4.9 Mummification

Figure 4.10 shows a Year 3 pupil's restructuring of information she had read in various sources about home life in Ancient Greek times. In this case the teacher had given her a pre-prepared grid to guide the collection of the information.

Work in the Home

Jobs done in the Home	Evidence Found	Who did the work
cooking	Statue	A woman maybe a Slave
washing	carving	A Slave or a woman
Sewing and mending	carving	A Woman maybe a Slave
get water	Picture	A woman or a slave
grilling meat	carving	A Slave or a Woman
Careing For children	Picture on a vors	A slave careing for children

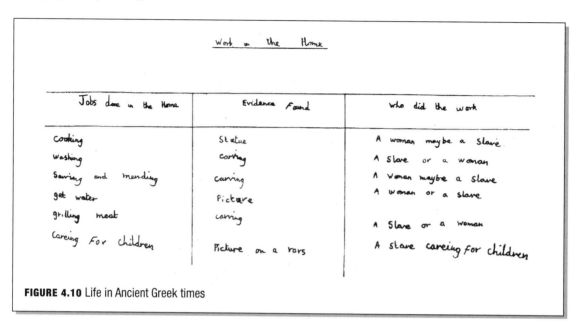

FIGURE 4.10 Life in Ancient Greek times

Later, the pupil wrote an account of what she had learnt from this experience (Figure 4.11).

working in the home

I found out that ladys do most of the work.

I found out that men are really lazy because they did nothing but sit around. There is no evidence of working in the house.

There was evidence of washing, cooking carrying, water, grilling meat and caring for children.

The ~~oth~~ evidence was carvings, statues and paintings.

Rachel

FIGURE 4.11 Gender roles in Ancient Greek times

Genre exchange

Restructuring can also take place by asking pupils to transpose something from one written genre into another. A group of ten-year-olds, for example, had read about scribes in Ancient Egypt. Normally, perhaps, they would simply have been asked to write about what they had read 'in your own words'. This would most likely have led to a good deal of copying of words and phrases from the original text. This time, however, they were asked to rewrite the information they had gathered into the form of a job advertisement. They examined advertisements in newspapers and an example of their writing is shown in Figure 4.12. As can be seen, it is unlikely that this was copied directly; instead, the children had had to read and understand the information.

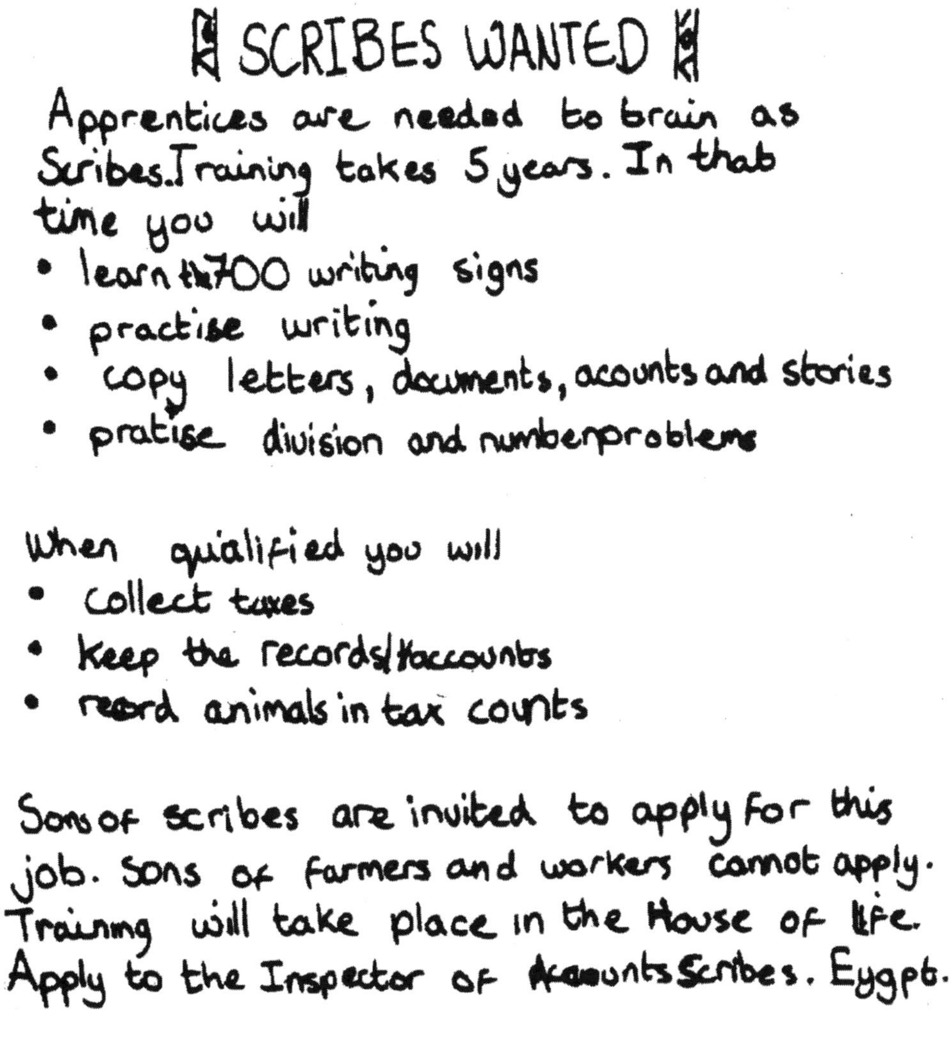
SCRIBES WANTED

Apprentices are needed to train as Scribes. Training takes 5 years. In that time you will

- learn the 700 writing signs
- practise writing
- copy letters, documents, acounts and stories
- pratise division and numberproblems

When quialified you will

- collect taxes
- keep the records/accounts
- record animals in tax counts

Sons of scribes are invited to apply for this job. Sons of farmers and workers cannot apply. Training will take place in the House of life. Apply to the Inspector of Acounts Scribes. Eygpt.

FIGURE 4.12 An advertisement for a scribe

This 'playing around' with genres not only forces children to reorganise their material – itself an aid to comprehension – but also gives them vital experience of the variety of genre forms, and guides them away from straight copying of information they have read. It is familiar to many teachers in the form of children using factual text to provide background details for fictional accounts. Figure 4.13 shows an example of this as one ten-year-old responds to her reading about the wives of Henry VIII.

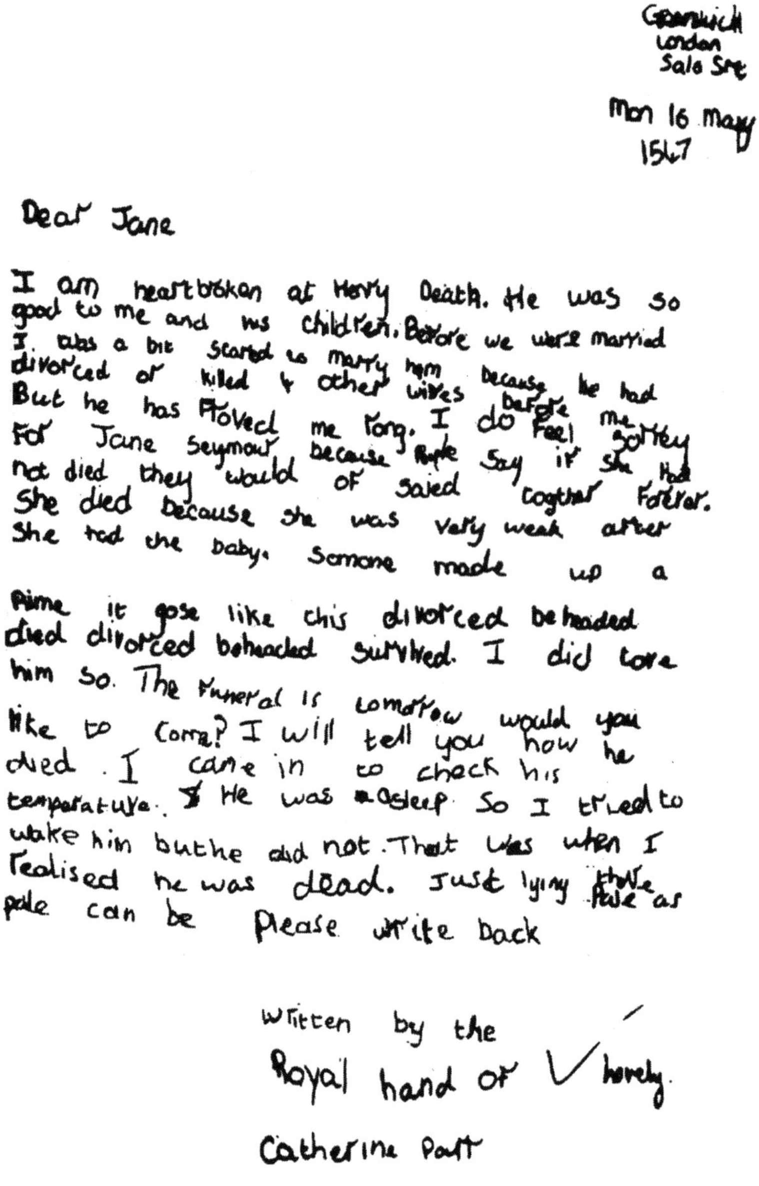

Greenwich
London
Salo Srt

Mon 16 May
1547

Dear Jane

I am heartbroken at Henry Death. He was so good to me and his children. Before we were married I was a bit scared to marry him because he had divorced or killed 4 other wives before me. But he has proved me rong. I do feel sorrey for Jane Seymour because pople say if she had not died they would of saied togther forever. She died because she was vary weak after she had the baby. Somone made up a rime it gose like this divorced beheaded died divorced beheaded survived. I did love him so. The funeral is tomorow would you like to come? I will tell you how he died. I cane in to check his temparature. He was asleep. So I tried to wake him but he did not. That was when I realised he was dead. Just lying there as pale can be. Please write back

Written by the Royal hand of lovely

Catherine Parr

FIGURE 4.13 A letter about Henry VIII's death

Conclusion

Interactive reading occurs just as much with the reading of non-fiction texts as it does with fiction. The assumption that the meaning of a text is somehow contained simply within the text, waiting to be grasped by the reader, has undoubtedly been partly responsible for the marked tendency of pupils to copy out chunks of information text. If the meaning is a given, there is little incentive for pupils to wrestle with the text trying to create it – all they need to do is extract the meaning; and writing down what the text says seems the obvious way of doing that. This chapter has suggested several approaches whereby the teacher might involve pupils in far more active and thoughtful ways than this of coming to grips with non-fiction texts. Common to all these teaching strategies is the conviction that meaning does not reside in a text but in what a reader makes of a text. Rosenblatt's (1978) concept of the 'poem' as the thread of meaning created as reader and text interact is just as relevant to non-fiction reading as it is to fiction.

Supporting writers

Introduction: how adults are supported in their writing

When adults write, they usually have access to a wide range of support. Think, for example, about young workers required to prepare a quote for a job for the first time. What support would they have in this situation?

1. Clear criteria for success

Before they start they know what they have to do and why. They have to specify what needs to be done, the materials to be used, the cost and the time it will take. It has to be priced low enough to get the job and high enough to make a profit.

2. Clear purpose and reader

They know why and to whom they are writing. This helps them make decisions about what information to include/exclude and the detail required.

3. Known consequences

They know what is going to happen to their writing. They find out how successful they have been because the client accepts or rejects the quote.

4. Access to models

They can see examples of others' attempts at similar tasks. They can see what information is provided and how it is set out.

5. Access to demonstrations

As apprentices they may have worked alongside other experienced tradespeople doing similar writing tasks. They will have seen the process of preparing and writing a quote.

6. Guidance during writing

An experienced colleague may 'walk them through' the whole process of preparing a written quote for a job. This person would highlight decisions that need to be made and offer advice on how to make them.

7. Access to guides for writing

Proformas may be provided by the employer stating explicitly what information is to be provided and how.

8. Provision of time

They get time to gather the information they need. They are not expected to work from memory. They may also be given a deadline for their final product. The ground rules are very clear.

9. Access to help

There is no penalty for going to others for assistance. In fact, this is expected. Suppliers will provide details required and workmates may pass on tips. When a problem arises, the writers go to a person who can provide solutions.

10. Immediate feedback

Through the questions they are asked about their writing they get feedback about any lack of clarity or information. They discover how well they have communicated.

Supports such as those listed above are available to adults no matter what kind of writing they are expected to produce. What did you do when you had to produce a job application for the first time, or the planning for a lesson or scheme of work, or a letter to parents or a pupil's end of year report? To what extent did you draw on the supports described?

For our everyday writing, such as letters to friends and shopping lists, support is rarely called upon because the tasks are relatively simple. Access to support becomes more important the more complicated or significant the writing and the more inexperienced the writer. It becomes crucial when the writing has really important consequences, such as a job application.

The implications for teaching

Adults are often faced with new writing challenges. Those who successfully meet these challenges have strategies for identifying and using the range of support available to them. Even the most experienced writers call on this support from time to time. The question is, 'Can teachers give pupils in classrooms the same support that is available to adults?'

Classroom research suggests that they can. As well as making writing tasks relevant, purposeful and satisfying, they can make explicit for pupils how written texts work, and how writers operate when writing particular texts.

In the rest of this chapter I will explore some of the strategies that teachers can use to do this, including:

1. providing models of writing and focusing pupils' attention on how these work;
2. demonstrating writing processes;
3. participating in writing tasks alongside pupils; and
4. scaffolding pupils in producing writing.

1. Providing and studying models of written work

'Show me some examples!' is a familiar request from people who are trying to learn new things. When learners are provided with examples, or models, of the kinds of written work they are asked to create, it offers them an opportunity to identify the distinctive features of the product. Often, if pupils are asked to explain how they tell the difference between one type of writing and another, they show very little explicit awareness of the features that distinguish these. Using models can help pupils identify the distinguishing characteristics of types of writing and can enable them to set specific goals for improving their writing or for monitoring and reviewing their efforts in a particular task. Through the examination of models, pupils get to see what it is that they need to learn to do. This strategy can be particularly valuable when they are asked to produce a type or style of writing that is unfamiliar to them, such as a business letter, a science report, a 'spooky' story or a compare-and-contrast essay.

There are a number of issues to consider when using models with pupils. The following guidelines will be useful when planning work with models so that pupils can apply what they learn to their own writing.

Models should be provided when pupils most need them

The best times to provide models are before pupils need to do a similar kind of writing themselves, or when they are having difficulties in their own writing. They are then able to see the activity as relevant to their learning needs. They will have an immediate opportunity to try some of the features of the models in their own writing.

Models should be complete texts

Pupils will benefit from seeing complete texts rather than extracts, so that they can discern overall structural, and organisational and formatting features. Where the focus is for the pupils to consider specific features of writing, such as the mechanics, it may be appropriate to provide copies of extracts after the entire text has been read aloud.

Models should be read aloud to pupils

If the teacher reads model texts aloud, this gives pupils the chance to familiarise themselves with the meanings of the text without having to do the hard, and distracting, work of decoding these texts for themselves. When they subsequently analyse the texts, the fact that they already know what these mean will be a major benefit since it allows them to concentrate on the job at hand.

Pupils need several models

Limiting analysis to just one text example does not allow pupils to decide which features of the model being used are critical. To take a very simple example, if pupils were presented with only one model of a newspaper birth announcement that happened to be written in a style that suggested the baby was 'writing', e.g. 'Hi, I'm Kylie Emma Smith and I was born on...', the pupils would have no way of knowing whether or not such a writing style was a critical characteristic of that form of writing. Presenting a range of birth announcements allows pupils to see that some features are critical, i.e. name, date of birth, parents' names, etc., and others, such as the style of writing, are not.

Looking at several models of the same kind of writing will also build pupils' awareness of the options and alternatives that writers have available to them. It also encourages pupils to view models as a resource they can use rather than as an ideal they must imitate.

Pupils should have individual copies of models

If the pupils have individual copies of each model, they are free to mark the text as necessary. For example, they might highlight main idea statements in one colour and supporting details in another. Alternatively, they may label parts of the text or write notes in the margin.

Pupils should be asked to develop lists of the features of a text

It is better to ask pupils to generate their own lists of features that describe how the models of writing work. Telling them exactly what they should find tends to constrain pupils' thinking and prevents them from drawing on their combined knowledge of how texts work. Finding out which features pupils automatically identify is also a useful way for the teacher to learn about their current understandings of, and strategies for, analysing and thinking about written texts. Pupils can, however, be invited to focus on general features, for example 'How have the writers structured their texts?' or 'How have they created a particular mood or atmosphere?' or 'How have they set out their letters?'

As an example of this process, Miss R's Year 5 class was beginning some work on writing instructional texts. She began by using as a model text a recipe for making pizza. After reading the text together the class discussed the following points (the key points that the teacher was trying to draw out are given in italics):

- How do you know this is a recipe? (*It tells you how to cook something. There's a list of ingredients.*)
- What kind of text is that? (*It tells you how to do something. Instructions.*)
- Can you think of any other texts that are like recipes and tell you how to do something? (*Rules for playing games. Instructions for fixing the computer.*)
- What does a recipe always begin with? (*There will always be a title. The title tells you what you are going to make.*)
- What does the first part of this recipe tell you? (*How big a pizza it will make. How long it takes.*)
- What does the next part tell you? (*The ingredients. What you need to make the pizza.*)
- How are the ingredients organised? (*A list. Measurements for each item.*)
- What follows the ingredients? (*What you have to do. The method.*)
- What do you notice about these directions? (*They are in the form of a numbered list. They use commands, or imperatives. They refer to time, either directly or by the use of chronological connectives, until, then etc.*)

Miss R then went on to ask her pupils to compile a checklist of the crucial features of a recipe. This was a useful learning activity in its own right as it forced the pupils to think abstractly about text features. It was also used later as an *aide-mémoire* when they came to write their own recipes. The questions Miss R used to prompt the pupils, together with some of the points she hoped they would notice and some of the answers they actually gave, are given in Table 5.1.

TABLE 5.1 Analysing a recipe

Thinking about recipes		
Questions the pupils were asked	**Teaching points**	**Some of the pupils' responses**
What comes first in a recipe?	The title of the dish The goal of the recipe	What you're going to make The name of what you're making
What comes next?	List of ingredients	What you need All your equipment and things
How are these laid out on the page?	Vertical list flushed left	A list
In what order are the ingredients listed?	This is debatable	The order in which you use them The biggest things first
What comes next in the recipe?	Directions for making the dish	What you have to do
In what order are these listed?	Chronological	The right order
Why?	Because that's how you use them	You'd get mixed up
How are they laid out on the page?	Usually a numbered list	Number of steps 1, 2, 3, 4 . . .
What tense are they written in?	Imperative	Do this . . .
Do they use passive or active verbs?	Active	You have to do actions
Who is the audience for a recipe?	There is an implied second person – an implied but not stated 'you'	Anyone making the dish The cook
What style of language would you expect?	Unembellished, businesslike, formal	Plain and simple
Why?	Ease of use – you need instant reference	It has to be quick to read

Pupils should work in groups

The most effective way for pupils to work in activities like this is when they collaborate in small groups or pairs. After they have been working in groups they can then be brought together for a report-back session with the whole class. Enlarged copies of the models on large sheets of paper or overhead projector transparencies can be useful when discussing and summarising group findings.

Pupils can help develop writing guides

An effective way of helping pupils make the connection between analysing models and their own writing is to develop writing guides with them. These guides remind pupils of the features they need to think about when they write. They can be displayed on a chart in the classroom or duplicated for pupils to use as they write. An example of a writing guide to help pupils structure their persuasive writing is given in Table 5.2.

TABLE 5.2 A writing guide for persuasive writing

What will your persuasive writing be about?	
Who is the audience?	
What will be the aim of your writing?	
What illustrations will you use?	
What layout will you use?	
What kind of sentences will you mostly use?	
List some of the words you might use	
alliteration	exaggeration
persuasive	rhyming

Other writing guides might be developed with pupils to identify features such as how writers create a particular atmosphere and mood, or how they develop characters in their work. These may take the form of lists of words and phrases pupils can use when they write, or a list of the characteristics that pupils need to include when they describe a character.

Writing guides can help pupils by:

■ removing some of the decisions pupils have to make as they write by providing a frame for pupils to plan and think about their writing as a whole;

■ helping them to set specific goals to achieve in a writing task; they can refer to the guide and ask themselves 'Does my writing have the features listed on the guide?';

■ helping them to solve writing problems independently; they can often find the help they need by referring to a guide instead of asking the teacher;

■ allowing them to provide specific help for each other; when pupils find it difficult to incorporate a particular feature of a guide into their writing they have, in effect, identified a writing problem and can seek specific help from their peers for solving it.

Guides also become a useful tool for discussing pupils' writing with them. One teacher described how she used the features lists developed by her pupils to guide her discussions with them about their writing.

> When I looked at the children's writing I used a photocopy of the features list we devised as a checklist to give them feedback. If an aspect on the list was included by a child I ticked the box. If there were omissions which should have been included I put a question mark. However, if the omission was allowable I put a dash in the box. I found this an extraordinarily simple way of providing feedback.

Developing writing guides with pupils gives them support to be successful in their writing. Pupils can use them as a resource rather than as recipes that must be followed slavishly. If they have access to several organisational or structural guides for particular types of writing they can select the form that best suits their ideas, purposes and audience.

2. Demonstrating writing processes

'Show me how!' is another familiar request from people learning something new. A demonstration by a proficient person offers learners insights into how they might do something themselves. But unlike many practical activities in the trades and the arts, the tools of the writer's craft are predominantly held in the head, not the hand. Consequently, much of what proficient writers do is not immediately accessible to learners. Although observers can see writers move the pen, pause and make changes to what has been written, the actual decisions they make and the way they make them remains hidden. As a result, people often believe that writing just happens – magically flowing from writers' minds onto the page. As one Year 3 child said, 'Writing is easy. You just get ideas in your head, then they come down into your shoulder and along your arm and on to the page'. Indeed, if pupils are asked what they think makes a good writer they may reveal misconceptions such as the following:

- the easier the writing flows onto the page the better writer you are;
- the work of writing is almost finished once the first draft is done;
- once a draft is done, all that is required is to correct conventional errors such as spelling and punctuation.

Pupils can be helped by the teacher demonstrating how he/she operates as a writer. This shared writing can be done by the teacher writing in front of pupils on large sheets of paper or on an overhead projector so that they can see the writing in progress. As the adult writes, he/she 'thinks aloud', giving pupils a running commentary on the thinking needed in order to write.

This is an ideal way of making the hidden thinking processes of writing explicit for learners. From these demonstrations pupils will be able to see that writing requires constant decision-making. They will see the adult confront problems about such things as topic, readership, ideas, organisation, language and conventions. They will also see how the adult manages this complex task by dealing, as much as possible, with one problem at a time. They will see him/her:

- selecting or clarifying the writing task;
- collecting and connecting information;
- gathering ideas and researching;
- planning;
- writing, reading and revising;
- doing final editing and proofreading;
- getting feedback.

What makes demonstration such a rich experience for pupils is the opportunity it provides for them to see the process of writing, not just the product of it. Pupils actually see why particular features of writing, such as spelling and grammar, are important to writers as well as when it is most appropriate to deal with them and how they can be dealt with. During a demonstration the pressure is off for pupils. They can focus on whatever is relevant to their writing needs.

Demonstrations can be given of any type of writing. Pupils are likely to appreciate seeing how an experienced writer tackles the kinds of tasks they are asked to do such as science reports, stories or history essays, especially if these are new or unfamiliar to them. Pupils can also learn a great deal by watching the adult work on writing tasks done for purposes beyond the classroom – that letter to the bank manager or to parents or to the editor of a newspaper. Pupils are often very interested in finding out what their teachers do when they write and they will try to use the strategies they have been shown in their own writing.

Demonstrations do not have to be time-consuming or complicated. Because they are intense observation activities, it is probably best not to spend more than 10 or 15 minutes at a time demonstrating. A short demonstration can be a routine feature of lessons or teachers can run a more intense series over a short period of time.

Sometimes, there may not be time in class to demonstrate the entire process of writing one text from beginning to end. Instead, what teachers can do is to demonstrate various stages in the process, doing some of the writing away from the pupils. This writing can then be shown to the pupils, with a brief explanation of how that stage in the task was reached, and time allowed for them to ask questions about it before the teacher goes on to demonstrate the next stage. For example, the teacher might demonstrate using a cut-and-paste strategy or ways of tackling planning of text. There may also be a focus on features of written products that are causing pupils difficulty, such as writing an effective conclusion to an essay or using quotation marks accurately.

To help pupils make the connection between demonstrations and their independent writing, it can be useful to develop process guides with them. Like the writing guides described earlier, process guides remind pupils of the problem-solving strategies they can apply while they are writing. These guides can also take the form of wall charts or duplicated sheets for pupils to use as they write. Typically, process guides are reminders of the sorts of questions successful writers ask themselves as they write, or as they re-read their writing in preparation for a second draft. For example, one teacher provided his Year 6 pupils with the process guide shown in Table 5.3. His pupils used this guide to self-monitor their writing processes before, during and after writing and as a discussion starter when they shared their writing with each other.

3. Participating in writing tasks alongside pupils

'Do it with me!' is yet another request likely to be heard when new things are shown and demonstrated to people. Novice writers often find it difficult to integrate effectively all they must think about and do as they write. As a result they can easily get stuck in writing ruts, focusing too much of their attention on the wrong issues at the wrong time. For example, pupils may give too much of their early attention to solving spelling problems, or they may focus too much on text structure before they have worked out what ideas and information they have to write about. The surprising thing is that even when pupils can talk sensibly about effective writing processes and product features, they may not be able to translate this easily into practice in their own writing. If the teacher participates with pupils as they attempt a new or difficult writing task, this can help them make the transition from knowing about writing processes and text features to actually being able to use this knowledge in their own writing.

When teachers participate with pupils in completing a writing task, the best role they can take is a guiding, supportive one. For example, they may take responsibility for scribing the text and guiding its production, although it is the pupils who are actually doing the composing. In this way both teacher and pupils participate in creating the written text and completing a task that the pupils may not normally be able to do successfully on their own. The idea is for the teacher to set up pupils to think and make writing decisions in collaboration with their peers, possibly with the occasional suggestion from above. This is what distinguishes this approach from process demonstrations where teachers show pupils how they make writing decisions. Through the questions posed and the input offered to the group, teachers can frame and guide pupils' thinking by making writing problems explicit, and challenge pupils to solve them.

TABLE 5.3 A writing process checklist

Before writing	Why do I want to write about this topic?	
	How will I develop my ideas?	
	Who will I discuss it with?	
	My initial plan is . . .	
	Who will read this piece?	
	What do I want it to do to/for them?	
During writing	Am I thinking about my reader by including: excitement, humour, suspense, my opinions?	
	Am I thinking about how this will end?	
	Will it help if I check out what I have written with someone else?	
After writing	Have my readers responded as I hoped?	
	Can I change the language to make it more effective?	
	What words are there that I have not used before in my writing?	
	My favourite sentence is . . .	
	Have I read the entire piece aloud to myself and to one other person?	
	Have I underlined words I think I may have misspelled?	
	Have I checked full stops, capitals and speech marks?	

Writing with pupils can, at times, be successful with large groups or even the whole class, but it probably operates best with a small group of about five pupils. This allows all members of the group actively to negotiate the making of the text – the central purpose of the activity.

Since teachers can usually write faster than any of the pupils, a useful role is to act as scribe. This frees the pupils to keep thinking while someone else does the physical writing. If this writing is done on large sheets of paper then everyone will be able to see it clearly and re-read it whenever they need to. The kinds of questions the teacher asks and the input he/she offers during a participatory writing activity are the keys to its success. For example, teachers can:

- ensure that the topic is one where the pupils share some knowledge or experience;

- make sure pupils are clear about the purpose of, and the likely readers for, the writing task from the beginning by asking 'What's our writing task? Why are we doing it? Who is going to read it? What do we need to tell our readers? What type of writing do you think will suit our purposes?';

- activate pupils' existing knowledge by recalling other occasions when they have written for similar purposes and readers, or by reviewing demonstrations, models and guides that they have seen and used;

- get pupils to brainstorm ideas and information for writing by asking 'What do you know about the topic?' If necessary, this can lead to further research to gather more information;

- help pupils think about ways of organising their 'brainstorm' list as a way of planning their writing: 'How can we organise our ideas? Can you group any together into categories? How will we begin our writing (report/essay/story etc.)?';

- help pupils draw on their existing knowledge and experience to solve writing problems that come up: 'Remember when we...? Can you do something similar here?';

- show pupils how to use writing and process guides they have developed in earlier activities as a resource for solving problems they encounter in their writing: 'Look back at...Is that guide any help to us now?';

- frequently re-read the developing text to the group to encourage pupils to monitor meaning and plan ahead before composing more text: 'How does what we have just written fit with our introduction?' or 'What do we need to include next?' Sometimes it may be necessary to go right back to the beginning of the text; at other times, re-reading only a few sentences when pupils are stuck will suffice;

- suggest solutions to problems from which they can choose the option they think is most appropriate: 'Some things you could do here are...Which one do you think would work best?';

- show pupils how different solutions might work in their writing; for example, teachers might try out different beginnings on scrap paper, re-organise an introduction so pupils can compare it with the original version, model alternative ways of expressing the same meaning etc.;

- take on the role of the reader for the pupils by pointing out any inconsistencies or vague meanings: 'If I were another pupil reading this I don't think I would understand what you mean by... Can you make it clearer?' or 'Can you expand on this point?' Teachers might also respond positively when the group has done something well: 'That makes it very clear; I know exactly what you mean there';

- allow pupils to 'think aloud' as they make suggestions to the group and help them to translate this into effective written language: 'Is that what you mean...? How could you write that down so your readers understand?';

- help pupils to clarify their understanding of the content or ideas they are writing about; sometimes pupils will reveal that their difficulties in solving a problem are not due to lack of writing ability but more to do with confused concepts or misinterpreted information; and, finally,

- involve pupils in making decisions about how the writing will be published and presented to intended readers and about how they will get a response to their work.

Teachers have a dual role when they participate in writing tasks with pupils. They are there not only to guide pupils through the process of writing but also to work at developing their group co-operation and discussion skills. Helping them to establish an effective pattern of interaction and collaboration on tasks with their peers can offer a model for working effectively in groups when the teacher is not present.

Pupils will engage more enthusiastically in a participatory writing activity when the writing task they are working on serves a clear purpose. The group may, for example, be working to research part of a topic being explored by the whole class. Their task for participatory writing could be that of writing a report of their research findings for other pupils in the class to read and learn from. Alternatively, a group may work with the teacher to produce a model essay for other pupils to respond to and discuss. Whatever the purpose, as long as pupils believe the task is likely to have satisfying consequences for them, they will probably try hard to do it well.

In collaboration, it can be difficult for the teacher not to make writing decisions for the pupils, especially when they suggest things which seem inappropriate. However, if teachers write or change the text without consulting the pupils who were responsible for it, this will lessen the learning opportunities for the pupils. The idea is for the pupils to participate in the decision-making so that they can operate more effectively on their own later. The teacher can alert them to any inappropriate decisions they may make by discussing an alternative point of view from a reader of the text. If, despite the advice of the teacher, the pupils do not choose the most appropriate option, this should be allowed to stand. In this way pupils can be shown that their viewpoints are taken seriously.

The teacher's role in participatory writing is to foster pupils' decision-making processes during writing. This can be a powerful strategy for helping pupils develop their knowledge of writing and writing processes.

4. Scaffolding pupils in producing writing

'Help me do it!' is also something that learners of a process often say as they take their first faltering steps. Think of babies who have witnessed countless people walking and are desperate to master this process for themselves, or young children who have seen older siblings ride their bicycles and want to copy, or children who have seen others swimming and want to do the same. In none of these cases can the learner simply move in one bound from observing demonstrations to performing the action completely independently. They need support – adult hands holding them up, allowing them to perform the action, and gradually, over time, withdrawing until independence is achieved. Learning to write is no different from these other actions – it needs the support of more accomplished practitioners to enable learners to be successful even in their early attempts. Some pupils will learn most of what they need to know about writing a particular kind of text from the demonstrations of writing they have experienced. For many, however, the jump from being shown how to write in a particular way to being able to write that way independently is simply too big for them to make easily. They need more support as they begin to learn to be independent writers.

This phase involves scaffolded writing, during which teachers can offer pupils strategies to aid their writing, which they can use without an adult necessarily being alongside them. One such strategy is the use of writing frames, which can act both as a way of increasing a pupil's experience of a particular type of writing and as a substitute for the teacher's direct interventions which encourage pupils to extend their writing.

A writing frame consists of a skeleton outline to scaffold pupils' writing of a particular text type. The skeleton framework consists of different key words or phrases, according to the particular generic form. The template of starters, connectives and sentence modifiers which constitute a writing frame gives pupils a structure within which they can concentrate on communicating what they want to say, rather than getting lost in the form. However, by using the form, pupils become increasingly familiar with it.

Some example writing frames are given in Tables 5.4 and 5.5, and further, photocopiable, examples can be found in Lewis and Wray (1997 and 1998).

Notice how writing with this kind of frame scaffolds writing in a number of ways:

(a) It does not present writers with a blank page. There is comfort in the fact that there is already some writing on this page. This alone can be enough to encourage weaker writers to write at greater length.

(b) The frame provides a series of prompts to pupils' writing. Using the frame is rather like having a dialogue with the page and the prompts serve to model the register of that particular piece of writing.

(c) The frame deliberately includes connectives beyond the simple 'and then'. Extended use of frames can result in pupils spontaneously using these more elaborate connectives in other writing.

(d) The frame is designed around the typical structure of a particular genre. It thus gives pupils access to this structure and implicitly teaches them a way of writing this type of text.

TABLE 5.4 An example writing frame

Before I began this topic I thought that . . .
But when I read about it I found out that . . .
I also learnt that . . .
Furthermore, I learnt that . . .
Finally, I learnt that . . .

The use of a frame should always begin with shared writing, discussion and teacher modelling before moving on to collaborative writing (teacher and pupils together) and then to the pupils undertaking writing supported by the frame. This oral, teacher modelling, joint construction pattern of teaching is vital, for it not only models the generic form and teaches the words that signal connections and transitions, but it also provides opportunities for developing pupils' oral language and their thinking. Some pupils, especially those with learning difficulties, may need many oral sessions and sessions in which their teacher acts as a scribe before they are ready to attempt their own writing.

It is useful to make 'big' versions of the frames for use in shared writing. It is important that the pupils understand that the frame is a supportive draft and words may be crossed out or substituted. Extra sentences may be added or surplus starters crossed out. The frame should be treated as a flexible aid not a rigid form.

TABLE 5.5 An alternative writing frame

Although I already knew that …
I have learnt some new facts. I learnt that …
I also learnt that …
Another fact I learnt was …
However, the most interesting thing I learnt was …

When the pupils have a purpose for writing, they may be offered a frame:

- when they first attempt independent writing in an unfamiliar text type and a scaffold might be helpful to them;
- when they appear stuck in a particular mode of writing, e.g. constantly using 'and then' when writing an account;
- when they 'wander' between text types in a way that demonstrates a lack of understanding of a particular type, e.g. while writing an instructional text such as a recipe they start in the second person ('First you beat the egg') but then shift into a recount ('Next, I stirred in the flour'); and
- when they have written something in one structure (often a personal recount) which would be more appropriate in a different form, e.g. writing up a science experiment as a personal recount.

Writing frames can be helpful to pupils of all ages and abilities. They are particularly useful, however, with pupils of average writing ability and with those who find writing difficult. It would, of course, be unnecessary to use the frame with writers already confident and fluent in a particular text type, but they can be used to introduce such writers to new types. The aim with all pupils is for them to reach the stage of assimilating the generic structures and language features into their independent writing repertoires. Pupils therefore need to use the frames less and less as their knowledge of a particular form increases. At this later stage, when pupils begin to show evidence of independent usage, they may need to have only a master copy of the frames available as help cards for those occasions when they need a prompt. A box of such help cards could be a part of the writing area in which pupils are encouraged to refer to many different aids to their writing. This is one way of encouraging pupils to begin to make independent decisions about their own learning.

Conclusion

What I have tried to do in this chapter is to put forward a model for the teaching of writing which is active and deliberate. Pedagogies for writing have been much slower to develop than for reading, and in the past teachers were sometimes given the impression that pupils' writing would simply develop given sufficient opportunity and motivation to write. Even major steps forward in thinking about writing in schools – such as the process writing movement of the 1980s – held within them the romantic notion that all young writers really needed to do was to discover their own writing voices.

The approach taken in this chapter is much more directive than that. Although voice and motivation are important ideas in writing, pupils still need to be taught how to create meaning within the commonly agreed frameworks that constitute writing in our particular culture. The approach outlined here could be termed an apprenticeship approach, being centralised as it is around the key idea of an expert writer (teachers) inducting novices (pupils) into his/her expert ways of acting. Teaching writing is conceived as shifting the burden of activity gradually from the expert to the novice, using scaffolding to ease the process of the novice becoming independent. This is a vision of teaching with enormous potential in all areas of learning.

Writing in science

Introduction

Pupils do a lot of writing in science lessons; they copy notes from the board, write up experiments, draw and label diagrams and write notes summarising ideas or work carried out in the lesson. It does seem to be the case, however, that a great deal of the writing asked of pupils in science lessons is of a fairly low level and undemanding nature. Osborne and Collins (2000) found that many 11-year-olds in secondary classrooms complained that they spent most of their time in science 'copying' from the board or a book, or from photocopied sheets. In our research in primary schools (Wray and Lewis 1992) we found a similarly high use of copying in science and in more general 'project' work. We did find many children who seemed to know perfectly well that they were not supposed to copy from books and could tell us that they had to write down the information they found 'in our own words'. This, unfortunately, often meant nothing more than changing individual words, a strategy which did not seem to push children towards making real sense of information they found and which, occasionally, led to them unwittingly changing the sense of what they wrote. An example of this was found in the work of one boy who read in a book about starfish, 'Its colour varies from brownish yellow to purple'. He wrote down 'The colour changes from brown to purple', and said 'I used different words so I wasn't copying'.

As an activity, there is now considerable research that shows that copying or undemanding writing activities are of little educational value. They are associated modes of teaching centred around the transmission of information – teachers, directly or indirectly, 'transmit' information which pupils 'receive' and learn. Research has suggested this mode to be the least effective in helping pupils to attain knowledge and understanding of a subject (Eggleston *et al.* 1976). 'Copying' is an activity in which little active processing or participation is required by the learner. Such work gives pupils little control over their own learning and ultimately leads to boredom and disenchantment.

Yet clearly writing is an essential part of science. The fact is that scientists write; otherwise scientific knowledge could not develop and spread. We do not, of course, expect our pupils to write scientific research papers but we should expect them to become familiar, even in simple forms, with some of the standard types of writing that are used in science. This will help them to engage with science as a 'real', challenging part of human life, rather than as the dull, fact-amassing subject it can sometimes seem in school. This chapter, therefore, explores the nature of writing in science and how writing can be given a more extended role in the process of learning science.

The nature of scientific text

Science tends to be characterised by the use of a style of writing with which most pupils will be unfamiliar. There is abundant evidence that the most familiar form of writing for pupils at any level of their schooling is that of the narrative. Children begin their writing careers by writing narratives. Later these become 'stories', and great store is set by pupils' abilities to write in this form. Narrative predominates in literacy work and in subjects such as history. There are good reasons for this. There is something distinctly human about telling each other stories. We use this language form to represent our experiences to ourselves and to others: we remember ideas and facts through the narratives they are linked to. There is a place for narratives in science, too, a point I will return to later in this chapter. But, in general, science is characterised by different writing forms.

First, science writing aims to be impersonal; that is it avoids mention of any particular person carrying out an action. The everyday language of 'My friend Alexander and I melted the ice cubes in the cup' becomes 'The ice was melted'. The personal agent of the action is removed, the passive rather than the active voice is chosen and details of setting are lost. Agents, active sentences and contextual details belong in narrative writing; scientific reports or explanations tend to remove these. It is generally argued that this is because science tries to portray itself as a source of objective knowledge. Narrative accounts are, in general, subjective accounts of experience and, therefore, science seeks to distance itself and portray the knowledge it offers as something which is a reflection of a real world which is independent of the observer.

Lemke (1990) has argued that the language of science uses a range of features which children generally find peculiar. It avoids colloquial forms (a scientist would never write 'the liquid phase didn't last long'); it uses unfamiliar technical terms such as 'molecule' and 'soluble', but also familiar words such as 'energy', 'force' and 'power' in unfamiliar ways. It avoids personality and figurative language (a scientist could not write 'I thought the effect of the melting was rather like moonlight shining on the water'). By doing this, science is aiming for a seriousness and an objectivity which exists above and beyond personal experience. But these features make learning scientific language rather like learning a foreign language and require the pupil to learn a new grammar and meaning-making system. In addition, science also employs symbols other than words to communicate its meaning, freely using a mixture of words, graphs, charts, diagrams, symbols, equations and pictures. As Lemke (1990: 139) points out:

> If some foreign languages are more difficult for you to learn than others, that is mainly because they are less like the language you already know, or the experiences you represent are less familiar. Science has its own distinctive genres, its thematic formations, its practical skills. In their forms they are no

more intellectually complex or difficult than those of any other subject. They are less familiar, less like what we are already used to.

Scientific writing offers some particular grammatical problems. One is the denser use of lexical items (words or phrases referring to content or factual knowledge) in science texts than in everyday language. For example, contrast the density of lexical items (shown in italics) in the following sentences:

We had to put the *ice* carefully in a *pot* and then we had to *melt* it slowly.

The *atomic nucleus absorbs* and *emits energy* in *quanta*, or *discrete units*.

The first sentence is typical of everyday language and contains only three lexical items. The second sentence on the other hand, very definitely scientific writing, contains eight. This much higher lexical density is typical of science text and contributes greatly to its reading difficulty.

A second common problem in science text is the use of grammatical metaphor, where one grammatical structure is replaced by another. The most common is nominalisation, where a noun is substituted for a verb or where nouns are used as adjectives. So instead of talking about 'how fast a car speeds up', we talk of the 'car's acceleration'; or instead of talking about 'how quickly cracks in glass grow', we talk about 'glass crack growth rate'. Scientific language is full of examples of this and the process of nominalisation is part of the attempt made by science as a discipline to objectify reality. The scientific world is full of objects and processes between which causal relationships are explored and defined, and the language used within the discipline helps to achieve this view of the world. It is also true, of course, that nominalisation generally cuts down on the wordage, serving its function of communicating complex ideas in an economic and efficient manner, but at the same time ensuring high idea density within the texts produced.

Part of the job of the teacher in a science lesson is to help pupils translate between scientific language and the everyday language with which they will be more familiar. Learning science is as much learning how to use the language of science as it is learning the facts and definitions of science or its experimental procedures. Learning a language requires opportunities to use that language and to write scientifically.

But what do scientists write? An important theme of this book is that learners, mostly, do not simply absorb knowledge about the texts they are required to read and write across the curriculum – they need to be taught this. A crucial step to take before planning such teaching is to elicit the main features of the types of text that get written within a subject. What, then, are the standard written forms in science? And how can pupils be helped to write in this manner?

The genres of science

Martin and Miller (1988) argue that the major genres of science are:

1. the report, which has four forms:
    - reports that classify;
    - reports that decompose, explaining the whole in terms of its constituent parts;
    - reports that describe functions and processes; and
    - reports that list properties;
2. explanations;
3. experimental accounts, which consist of:
    - procedural texts explaining how to do experiments;
    - recounts of experiments that have been conducted; and
4. exposition which presents arguments in favour of a position.

Reports

Reports are very much a feature of biology, while explanations tend to predominate more in the physical sciences. Helping pupils to understand and write these kinds of reports requires an awareness of their main structures.

Usually, reports use generic participants[1] such as 'plants', 'animals', 'ecosystems'; they tend to use timeless verbs in the simple present tense, such as 'shows', 'have', 'consists of'; and they use a large number of clauses containing words like 'is', 'have' and 'are', which are used to associate properties with the objects or phenomena. There are several sub-types of report.

Classification reports

These begin with an opening, general classification, for example, 'a whale is a mammal which lives in the sea', or, 'plants are divided into a number of groups'. They then provide a description of the phenomenon, which includes some or all of its:

- qualities: 'because it is a mammal it is warm blooded'; 'algae are simple plants';
- habits and/or behaviour: 'it eats plankton from the sea and communicates with other whales by making sounds'; 'fungi and algae are able to feed on other plants and animals'; and
- functions: 'the hole on the top of the whale is to allow it to breath air'; 'fungi and algae live together to help each other'.

---

1 The term 'noun' would be used here in traditional grammatical analysis. Genre theory, which underpins analyses of text types like those I am presenting here, is based upon functional grammar which uses different terminology and, in this case, would substitute the term 'participant'. If our focus is to analyse the function of particular elements within texts, which it is here, then 'participant' will be the preferred term. Thus, the sentence 'Copper sulphate is a blue, crystalline substance' has two participants: 'Copper sulphate' and 'a blue, crystalline substance'. In traditional grammar these would be termed 'noun phrases'.

Decomposition reports

These begin with an opening, general statement, for example, 'the heart is the organ responsible for pumping blood around the body'. They then provide a description of the various parts and their functions: 'it consists of four chambers – the right atrium, the left atrium ... In the right atrium...'.

Descriptive reports

These begin with an opening, general statement, for example, 'the lungs are where gaseous exchange takes place'. They then contain a set of statements of its various functions: 'oxygen is absorbed from the air'.

Reports listing properties

These begin with an opening, general statement, for example, 'all living things have the following properties'. They then contain a list of the properties: movement, nutrition, reproduction etc.

Explanations

Scientific texts contain a large number of explanations – explanations of how the heart works, what happens when elements combine, how stars are formed or why we believe the surface of the Earth consists of plates. Explanations differ from reports in two main ways: they tend to have a higher proportion of action verbs (water *evaporates*, atoms *combine*, plates *collide*); and these actions are organised in a logical, usually causal, sequence. They will be characterised by a mixture of chronological (*first, next, afterwards, subsequently*) and causal (*because of this, therefore, as a result*) connectives.

Explanations are usually structured into two main sections. First, there will be a general statement to introduce the topic: 'All matter can be found in three forms – solid, liquid or gas'. This will be followed by a series of logical steps explaining how or why something occurs. These steps continue until the final state is produced or the explanation is complete:

> Matter is made of tiny particles. In a solid, these are tightly held in fixed positions and can only vibrate, which makes the shape of the matter difficult to change. When the matter is heated, this causes the atoms which make it up to vibrate more strongly and therefore break free of their fixed position. The matter thus becomes liquid. When it is heated still more the atoms break totally free and move very far apart from each other, turning the matter into a gas. When the gas is cooled the atoms slow down their vibrations, turning the matter back to a liquid and then, eventually, a solid.

Experimental reports

This is the most familiar genre of science writing to both pupils and teachers. Experimental reports have quite a standard structure: Aim – Method – Results – Conclusions. This structure is found at all levels, from early experimental reports written by primary school pupils to very sophisticated, science research reports written by laboratory scientists. The aim of the report is to establish the purpose of the experiment described, then to give a description of the methods used so that the experiment could be replicated by others, then to present the data that were collected during the experiment, and to conclude by offering an interpretation of the data – relating the conclusions to the original aims.

One of the most difficult features of this style of writing for most pupils is the use of the passive voice. So rather than using the active, saying 'we heated the liquid', science reports tend to say 'the liquid was heated'. The reason for using such language is that, in science, the object of interest is the liquid not the scientists who heated it. The language of science supports the view inherent in the discipline that reality is objective, existing in its own right without the interpretations of humans. Of course, this positivist philosophy in science has been challenged: many scientists would now accept a more subjective account of the created world. The language of science has not, however, changed much, and if the aim of science teaching is to begin the process of making pupils scientifically literate – able to read and write at least basic science – then the pupils must be taught how to write in the standard genres.

Argument and exposition

This is a genre rather less used in science, especially in the school books designed to help teach science, which claim to report unequivocal and uncontested fact. In science outside schools, however, argument is a very important part of the writing of scientists. Popular writing in science, such as Richard Dawkins's *The Selfish Gene*, for example, contains carefully constructed arguments for a particular interpretation, in this case of evolution. Scientists who have developed new ways of looking at the world – the Darwins, Einsteins and Newtons etc. – have also used writing as their principal means of convincing an often sceptical fraternity of fellow scientists that their interpretation is the correct one. Other scientific argument deals with the question of 'how we know'. Such writing foregrounds the processes of science rather than its 'facts', and explores the means by which science develops its knowledge.

Constructing an argument for any scientific assertion requires the use of evidence and the consideration of counter-arguments. Writing of this type will tend, therefore, to consist of a number of assertions, each of which is backed up by an elaboration of the reasons in favour of accepting it and a dismantling of reasons why it should not be accepted. The structure will thus be: assertion; point; counterpoint.

Arguments will also include lots of logical connectives which relate claims to the evidence underpinning them. Words such as 'because', 'consequently', 'therefore' etc. are characteristic of such writing.

In addition to its role in furthering debate in the discipline of science, argument and its characteristics also reflects what is perhaps the most important feature of science writing, that is the process of reasoning from evidence to conclusions. The very essence of what scientists do is to gather evidence and use it to support conclusions about aspects of the physical world. Such conclusions are generally not self-evident or inescapable and scientists must in their writing present an argument as to why their conclusions are the most acceptable or likely. Virtually all science writing, therefore, contains elements of argument.

Narrative writing in science

In one sense, science writers are all tellers of stories – narratives about elements of the world and how it works. Popular knowledge of science relies on narrative accounts, often written by people (e.g. Stephen Hawking, Richard Dawkins) who have made significant contributions to expanding scientific knowledge. Rather than using the normal discourse of science with its graphs, diagrams, illustrations and mathematics, they rely on word-based, narrative accounts of phenomena and their discovery, often using some or all of the essential narrative elements – plot, voice, scene, agents, an end and a sense of audience – which have been carefully removed from normal scientific text. These popularisers produce science as literature, and their works are judged as literary artefacts as well as on the quality and accuracy of their scientific content.

Does narrative writing, then, have any value in school science? It is true that the difficulties of writing in the formal 'scientific' style described earlier may discourage many pupils from writing at all in science. If we want to engage pupils with ideas in science, it might be sensible to offer writing activities which do not cause so many difficulties. Using a familiar genre will at least begin the process of helping pupils express their thoughts in written language. This suggests that, at least early on in their experience of science, pupils might benefit from being allowed and encouraged to write in a narrative style. After all, we do not want to dampen the enthusiasm of pupils like nine-year-old Alexander who wrote, after taking part in a science experiment:

> So we took the blue sparkly diamonds and Mr Jones heated them really fiercely. Do you know what happened? They all went white! We were very excited and Emma Watts asked if that would happen to her mum's ring. Mr Jones said it only worked with some gems.

It is clear, however, that this kind of writing, important as it may be for learners at a certain stage of their understanding of science, can only be a temporary phenomenon. Everyday language and genres do not, in the end, work well in science, so we must take pupils beyond them by teaching the conventions of the scientific genre, transforming their personal experience into a communicative form which represents knowledge to others. Developing this sense of scientific genre means exploring the differences between scientific forms of writing and other forms of writing. A useful way to engage pupils in this is to ask them to write about their science for a range of different purposes and audiences. They might, for example, write for different audiences:

- for a friend who missed the lesson in school;
- for their mother to explain what they did in school today;
- as a letter to a pen-pal;
- for a younger pupil to explain why science is fascinating; or
- as a poster for a parents' evening.

They might also write about the science:

- as a poem;
- as an article for a school magazine;
- as a set of instructions for someone else to do the experiment;
- as an article in the *Sun* newspaper;
- as an entry in their diary;
- as a piece of narrative verse;
- as a time traveller from the sixteenth century;
- as part of a science fiction story; or
- as a poster for the school hall.

It is important to remember, however, that these styles of writing are not scientific writing, and that regular use of this approach is only a staging post *en route* to inducting pupils into genuine science writing. It could be argued that one of the functions of scientific teaching is to introduce beginners to the standard forms of writing science. Although many teachers would claim that the formal genres of science are too hard for pupils, especially primary pupils, there are a number of strategies available for scaffolding learners in these conventions and forms.

Teaching writing in science

The important point here is that such writing skills will not be acquired unless they are specifically taught. Moreover, they will not be understood unless the need for the requirements is specifically explained to pupils.

An effective approach to this teaching should be guided by the principles discussed in the previous chapter. Pupils need first to have plenty of good examples of the style of writing put before them. These can often show much more powerfully than the words or explanations of the teacher what is required in writing of this type. Thus, teachers need to find examples of real world science writing to display around the classroom. They should also select good efforts by pupils to place on the walls, or to read aloud to the rest of the class. Perhaps the most powerful teaching, however, occurs when the teacher actively models the process of science writing, composing a science report in front of the class, or working through a writing frame together with pupils. Writing frames (Lewis and Wray 1997) are simply scaffolds which provide important clues about how to organise the writing and the style of writing required. The frame guides the writer to the key features of the genre and is a planning tool used to organise the writing.

Writing of any quality requires planning and drafting – it is not simply acquired by osmosis but must be taught, and time must be given to developing the skills. Using a frame such as that shown in Figure 6.1, pupils' ideas can be discussed and used to co-construct an account on the board or OHP so that pupils can see a good example of how to write in this style. Once their confidence and understanding has developed, the frames can be used as an advance organiser for their writing. In the end, the teacher would hope that the frames could be disposed of altogether, as the standard characteristics of the genre become second nature.

Although	and	
are both		they are different in many ways.
(One)	has	
whilst	has	
They are also different in that		
Another way they are unalike is		
Finally		

FIGURE 6.1 A science report writing frame

Conclusion

This chapter has tried to show that writing in science is not something which is peripheral to the learning of science. Instead, writing in science is essential to developing scientific literacy – an understanding of how to read science, how to write science and the content of science itself. Developing pupils' abilities requires explicit teaching of the conventional structures of science writing and a range of exemplars of good practice. Worksheets that require little more than short phrases for completion do little to develop such knowledge and skills.

Writing in mathematics

Introduction

I began the previous chapter by making the point that pupils write all the time in science lessons. Mathematics lessons are no different, although there are clearly differences in the kinds of writing that are expected of pupils. Of course, the principal purpose of writing in mathematics will usually be to record the working out of mathematical problems and will probably feature the writing of numbers rather than text. There are other purposes for writing, however, and perhaps there needs to be an enhanced role for writing within the teaching and learning of mathematics. Some of these purposes might be:

- to plan and record mathematical investigations;
- to predict mathematical outcomes;
- to recount mathematical work of various kinds, including calculations;
- to give instructions for carrying out mathematical procedures; and
- to offer a detailed proof of a mathematical phenomenon.

This chapter will explore in more detail the characteristics of written mathematical texts and what might be expected of learners in the subject. It will go on to suggest approaches to teaching writing within mathematics.

The mathematics register

The very mention of the phrase 'the language of mathematics' suggests that there is a single set of characteristics which can be listed and applied. This is rather simplistic. Just as there are a number of activities that can be labelled as mathematics (including academic mathematics, school mathematics, recreational mathematics etc.), there are a variety of genres of text that may be called mathematical (e.g. a research paper, a textbook, an examination question and answer, a puzzle etc.). Each of these activities and genres will have some distinctive characteristics of their own, and there are, for example, some features of the genre of academic mathematics research papers that we would be surprised to see appear in a primary pupil's report of some investigative work. It seems likely, however, that any text that is identifiable as mathematical will share at least some linguistic characteristics with other texts that are also considered to be mathematical.

The linguistic features that contribute to identifying a text as mathematical include its vocabulary, its grammatical structure and the forms of argument it uses. A number of authors have given descriptions of the general features of mathematical texts. Halliday (1974) introduced the use of the concept of a mathematical 'register' to discussions about language in mathematics education contexts and provided an overview of some of the grammatical characteristics of such a register. This has been elaborated, from a mathematics education perspective, by Pimm (1987).

The most obvious characteristic is the use of a symbolic system completely different from that found in everyday written English. Many mathematical texts are full of 'sentences' like:

$$(a^2 + b^2)/3c = \sqrt{(x-y)}+z^2$$

This feature has led to the language of mathematics being described as 'a foreign language' (Ervinck 1992), and, when it is combined with the use of specialist vocabulary to name specifically mathematical objects and concepts (radius, sum, integer, tangent, hypotenuse), it is not surprising that learners find the reading and writing of mathematical text difficult. While the use of symbols and specialist vocabulary are perhaps the most visible aspects of many mathematical texts, they do not provide a full description of the nature of these texts. It is also necessary to look beyond the level of vocabulary at the syntax of the text and at the structures which serve to construct mathematical arguments.

Other features that have been identified as characteristic of much mathematical language include its 'density and conciseness...which tend to concentrate the reader's attention on the correctness of what was written rather than on its richness of meaning' (Austin and Howson 1979: 174). Like the scientific texts discussed in the previous chapter, mathematics texts, in general, have a high 'lexical density', that is a high ratio of 'content' words to 'grammatical' words.

Mathematics language also uses distinctive grammatical structures such as conditional phrases ('if...then...'), and hypothetical imperatives ('Let $a = 3$...'), one of the problems with which is the difference in usage and meaning of these structures from that found in everyday language. Readers and writers of mathematical text need first to 'tune in' to the genre, that is recognise it as different from their normal language.

Mathematics texts

There is, of course, substantial diversity between the forms of language used in different mathematical contexts, and it is not clear that the idea of a single mathematical register is sufficient to cope with the variation of functions and meanings to be found, for example, in a primary school textbook and in an academic research paper. Not only does the subject matter vary but also the modes of argument used in these discrete domains of mathematical activity are likely to differ substantially. Yet one of the aims of school mathematics teaching is to produce learners who, eventually, can understand and produce the mathematics writing that mathematicians deal with. So what does this writing look like?

Academic mathematics texts

The academic mathematics research report may be seen as the 'adult' equivalent of the investigation report. Even though mathematics writing is closely identified with a distinct symbol system, most guidelines and advice for writers of mathematics suggests that some 'natural language' is required to supplement the symbols (e.g. Gillman 1987; Knuth *et al.* 1989). The reasons given by these authors for including non-symbolic elements in mathematical texts, however, suggest that they are chiefly to make the text easier to read, particularly to an audience beyond the very small group of colleagues working in the same field, rather than to contribute to its meaning.

It is generally accepted that both scientific and mathematical texts are impersonal and formal. Clearly, the symbolic content discussed above contributes to this, but there are also a number of contributory characteristics of the 'natural' language, such as high modality (i.e. a high degree of certainty and an absence of such human frailties as doubt or expressions of attitude). Another source of this formality, as with science texts, is the use of nominal rather than verbal expressions. In statements such as: 'The demand that one angle of the isosceles triangle be equal to 90° means that...', the use of nominalisation separates the reader from the source of the 'demand'. This is represented as an abstract entity whose independent existence has important consequences. The ability to represent processes as objects, and hence to operate on the processes/objects themselves, is part of the power of mathematics; at the same time, it increases the impersonal effect, strengthening the impression that it is these processes/objects that are the active participants in mathematics rather than human mathematicians.

Looking beyond the level of individual symbols, words or even more complex phrases or statements, it also seems that the structure of extended sections of texts, in particular the ways in which arguments are constructed, are distinctive in mathematics. In academic mathematics a very high value is placed on deductive reasoning as a means of both 'discovering' knowledge and providing evidence for it. The linguistic structure of mathematical texts reflects this, especially in texts such as formal mathematical proofs. This text type is a standard component of most formal mathematical texts above school level (and in some school texts as well) but it can also cause even advanced learners considerable difficulty. In analysing the structure of proofs, writers (e.g. Konior 1993) have pointed out the importance of linguistic signals which mark the beginning ('It remains to show that...') and end ('Whence formula (24) follows') of phases in the argument. Konior suggests that expert readers make use of these signals to structure their reading of the whole text, but that beginning readers may not appreciate the function of such phrases. Equally, it is likely that beginning mathematical writers may not know how to make use of them effectively.

The characteristics of academic mathematical texts, outlined briefly above, form part of the background to the consideration of mathematical writing in school. While school pupils themselves are unlikely to come across such texts, they do form part of the experience of mathematics teachers and textbook writers and, as such, influence the texts encountered by pupils in school and the values placed by teachers on various forms of writing.

School mathematics texts

School mathematics texts have been thoroughly examined in terms of the difficulties they create for pupils in understanding their meanings. Shuard and Rothery's (1984) classic study identified difficulties associated with these textbooks' use of graphical elements and the layout of their pages, as well as their vocabulary and symbolism, any of which might contribute to a pupil's inability to make sense of the mathematics within them. Although it is possible to criticise the conciseness and formality of these textbooks because of the difficulties that they may cause learners, it is also the case that such books form a very large part of most pupils' (and their teachers') experience of mathematical text. Characteristics of their language are likely, therefore, to influence pupils writing in mathematics.

Like academic mathematical texts, school texts have a heavy symbolic content, although the range of symbols they contain is likely to be more limited. In addition, most school mathematics texts are heavily graphical and include tables, graphs, diagrams, plans, maps and pictures. It is probably the case, however, that these graphical elements are mostly 'decorative' (Shuard and Rothery 1984: 47) rather than 'mathematical'.

Such decorative features are also characteristic of the text in school mathematics books, as well as the graphics. As Kane (1968) points out, school texts tend to use a conventional and repetitive structure, in particular those sections containing examples and exercises. One of the effects of this, which may well be deliberate on the part of textbook producers, is to make the mathematics in the books easily accessible to pupils, without them being distracted by having to decipher unfamiliar text structures before getting to the mathematics. While this undoubtedly eases teachers' lives (pupils who grasp quickly what they have to do in the mathematics are less likely to ask irritating questions), it does little to induct pupils into the typical characteristics of mathematics writing.

As we saw with science in the previous chapter, there are some distinctive characteristics of mathematics writing with which we would hope that our pupils, eventually, become familiar. Again, as with science, writing in mathematics is closely bound up with learning mathematics and the development of mathematical literacy. Developing pupils' ability requires explicit teaching of the conventional structures of mathematical writing and a range of exemplars of good practice. Given the remarks above about school mathematics texts, it is unlikely that experience of these alone will be sufficient to produce pupils who can move towards writing mathematics like mathematicians. For this they need more targeted teaching.

Before exploring strategies for accomplishing this, we need to spend a little time looking at another important line of development in thinking about the role of writing in mathematics. It has been suggested that, in mathematics as in other subjects, writing in a subject is an important means of learning in that subject.

Writing to learn in the mathematics classroom

Recent years have seen increasing interest in communication in the mathematics classroom. In tandem with the move towards constructivist views of learning, pupils have begun to be given a role as producers of mathematical language rather than just as consumers. Attention has moved towards consideration of the roles that talking and writing may play in pupils' learning of mathematics.

The role of talking in learning mathematics has received a good deal of attention, with many suggestions for ways that teachers might encourage talk in their classrooms (e.g. Brissenden 1988; Mathematical Association 1987). The place of writing, however, is rather less well established. Supporters of 'Writing-to-Learn' in mathematics have suggested that writing should be part of investigations, claiming that writing can help pupils in their learning of mathematics, in particular in developing reflection and problem-solving processes.

Traditionally, very little writing, other than symbolic notation, has taken place in mathematics classrooms. The classic studies of writing in secondary classrooms in England and Wales (Britton *et al.* 1975; Martin *et al.* 1976) and in Scotland (Rogers and MacDonald 1985) found too little writing taking place in mathematics lessons for it to be worth analysing. These studies are dated but they indicate the traditional background of a lack of independent mathematical writing in secondary classrooms. Primary school evidence is even harder to come by, but the findings of Marks and Mousley (1990) in Australia are likely to be typical. They found a limited range of writing being used and, even where teachers claimed to be committed to the idea of increasing opportunities for their pupils to use language in the classroom to develop and communicate their mathematical understanding, pupils generally only wrote in a recount genre rather than in specifically mathematical styles.

More recently, there has been a development from the idea of 'Writing across the Curriculum', which focused on the development of writing through its use in various curriculum areas, towards the idea that writing is a useful intellectual tool for helping learning in all areas of the curriculum. Writing is seen to share a number of the characteristics of successful learning – that is it integrates hand, eye and brain in the quest to represent reality; it compels the reformulation of ideas ('thinking at the point of utterance' in James Britton's words); and it is audience-focused. As the writer struggles to represent ideas in a manner comprehensible to an outside reader, he/she is forced to clarify these ideas for him/herself.

On this basis it is argued that writing supports learning. Some of those arguing for the use of writing in mathematics classrooms have seen a special relationship between writing and mathematics. Emig's (1983) definition of 'clear writing' as that which 'signals without ambiguity the nature of conceptual relationships, whether they be co-ordinate, subordinate, superordinate, causal, or something else' (p. 127) suggests a concern with precision and with relationships that parallels that in mathematics.

There is evidence to support the relationship between writing and learning in mathematics. One study (Williams 2003), for example, placed students in control and experimental groups for the purpose of researching writing and problem-solving. Each group was taught a number of mathematical strategies and processes, and they were then each given problems to complete. The experimental group was asked, in addition, to write a few sentences about how they solved their problems; the control group was not required to write about their processes at all. The results showed that the students in both groups made progress in mathematical problem-solving, but that the students in the experimental group had learnt to solve the problems using more appropriate strategies at a faster rate than students in the control group. Being forced to express their thinking in writing seemed to have helped students in the experimental group to understand the mathematics they were engaged with.

In addition to claims that writing can enhance learning in a subject like mathematics, a major reason for enhancing the role of writing is that it might improve pupils' attitudes towards mathematics and thus remove one of the obstacles to their learning. Some writers (e.g. Borasi and Rose 1989) have suggested that writing texts such as journals can have a therapeutic effect and can help change pupils' perceptions of mathematics.

Writing has also been seen as essential in investigative work in mathematics. Mason *et al.* (1985), for example, argued that recording the problem-solving process and subsequently writing it up for someone else to read can both play a role in developing mathematical thinking about the problem and its solution. They propose a set of self-monitoring prompts to writing during problem-solving which provide 'a framework for organizing, recording, and creating mathematical experiences' (p. 22).

What do pupils write in mathematics?

Several teachers and researchers have suggested that writing should play a greater role in classroom mathematics work. There is little agreement, however, about what exactly pupils should write, and when teachers read pupil texts they may well have unspoken (and probably unconscious) assumptions about the forms of language that are 'appropriate'. As Kress (1990) argues, unless these assumptions are made explicit, some pupils are likely to be disadvantaged because their lack of facility with the language is interpreted as lack of knowledge of the subject content.

In spite of the substantial amount of work describing the use of writing in the mathematics classroom, there has been relatively little analysis of the texts produced. One secondary school study (Clarke *et al.* 1993) looked at the journals written in mathematics lessons. They found three main types of text produced within these journals which they labelled 'recount', 'summary' and 'dialogue'. These text types were seen as a hierarchy, with the dialogue being the most highly valued in terms of its representation of learning as active and enquiring, while the other two merely stated knowledge unproblematically.

Teaching writing in mathematics

In order that teachers should be able to help their pupils develop forms of written language that are acceptable within mathematics, these teachers must themselves have explicit knowledge of the appropriate forms of writing. This is true whether teachers decide to focus on pupils writing in mathematics as a form of apprenticing these pupils in formal, academic mathematical writing, or on pupils using writing as a medium of learning about mathematics.

As with the teaching of all forms of writing, pupils' experiences must begin with immersion in the forms required. They need to read and have read to them plenty of examples of mathematical writing. They also need to consider these texts in detail, deconstructing them and examining their grammatical features. There is no reason, for example, why mathematics writing should not have a place in shared reading sessions, where its distinctive structures, syntax and vocabulary can be explicitly discussed and clarified. As an example of this, consider the text shown in Figure 7.1.

Looking at the equals sign

The symbol '=' was first used in 1557.

It was the invention of an Englishman named Robert Recorde, the man who first introduced algebra to England. Recorde used the symbol ‖ in his 1557 book *The Whetstone of Witte*. He was simply trying to avoid having to write over and over again 'is equal to'.

But the symbol did not become popular right away. Some people preferred to carry on writing 'equals' as 'is equal to', while some others used the abbreviation *ae* or *oe* (for the Latin *aequalis* or 'equal'). This went on until well into the 1700s.

As for Recorde himself, he died in prison, where he had been sent as a debtor.

We can think of the equals sign as being like the middle of a pair of scales which balance perfectly. Everything on one side of the scales has exactly the same value as everything on the other side. So:

$$10 + 6 = 4 + 12$$

Ten added to six makes 16. Four added to 12 makes 16. So both sides balance.

This fact can help us work out things we might not otherwise know. So:

$$3a + 6 = 12$$

Both sides of the '=' are the same as each other, so if we take six away from both sides they will stay the same as each other:

$$3a = 6$$

Now we divide each side by 3. Each side will still be equal to the other.

$$a = 2$$

We have now identified the value of *a*.

FIGURE 7.1 A shared reading text for mathematics

During a shared reading session the following points might be discussed with the group:

- This is an example of an information report. Reports give information about particular topics. They will usually begin with a sentence or paragraph introducing the topic of the report and be followed by several details about the topic.

- The first half of this text is written in the past tense. The second switches to the present tense. Why are these different tenses used? In the first half, the purpose of the text is to tell the reader about something which happened in the past. In the second half the focus shifts to a description of the purpose of the equals sign.

- Look at the second part of the second sentence ('the man who…'). This has its own verb ('introduced') so it is a clause. What is its function in this sentence? It tells us more about Recorde. We call it an adjective clause because it describes a noun. Find some more examples of adjective clauses in the rest of the passage, that is groups of words, containing a verb, which describe a person or thing. Another example is: 'where he had been sent as a debtor'.

- Notice that sometimes these clauses are separated from the rest of the sentence by a comma, but sometimes they are not. Try removing the comma, or putting one in, and see what difference this makes to the meaning of the sentence.

- Investigate the meaning of the word 'equal'. This has a very specific meaning in mathematics that is different to its meanings in everyday language. Get the pupils to think of other meanings, for example: 'All men are created equal'; 'I am rather worried about going. Equally, it could be a good idea'.

It will also be beneficial for the teacher to exemplify mathematical writing by composing examples in shared writing sessions. A useful time to demonstrate investigative report writing, for example, would be after the group had completed an investigation in mathematics and were later to write their own reports of this. The teacher could, with help from the pupils, compose an example report on an overhead projector or interactive whiteboard. In the course of this, several important points could be discussed including:

- How should the report begin?
- What tense should it use?
- Should it mention the people who carried out the investigation by name, or should it talk about 'we'? Are there other ways of recounting what happened? What about using the passive?
- How should the report be structured? Should it use numbered sections, bullet points, or simple paragraphs?
- At which point should the report say what the investigation found?

Pupils will also benefit from some scaffolding support for their mathematics writing. Figure 7.2 shows a writing frame which some pupils might find useful for structuring their writing in advance of carrying out an investigation.

Mathematics: Planning and prediction

I have been asked to investigate

I already know that

So I will investigate by

I think I will find that

FIGURE 7.2 A mathematics writing frame

Conclusion

In this chapter I have explored the nature of writing in a number of mathematical contexts. While many mathematics teachers are suspicious about focusing upon pupils' writing in their subject, there is sufficient evidence available to suggest that this could be a beneficial move, not least in the support which writing in a subject gives to learning in that subject.

Mathematics writing is not natural; it needs teaching if pupils are to be able to write in a manner resembling that of mathematicians. Teaching writing in mathematics is, I would argue, no different from teaching writing in any subject, and aspects of the teaching model explored in Chapter 5 are equally relevant here. Teachers of all subjects, at all levels, could benefit from considering their pupils as apprentice writers in the subject, and using apprenticeship teaching strategies.

CHAPTER

8

Developing a critical approach to texts

Why is a critical approach important?

I was recently working with a Year 6 class on a history project about the Second World War. Among various investigations we pursued, one group were set the task of gathering information about the Holocaust. As well as collecting some suitable books from the class and school libraries, they also spent some time on the internet-connected computer in the school library. Among the texts they brought back from this particular experience was the following (I give only the first two paragraphs of a much longer document):

A short introduction to the study of Holocaust revisionism

Arthur R. Butz

[This article was originally published in the Daily Northwestern of May 13, 1991, corrected May 14]

I see three principal reasons for the widespread but erroneous belief in the legend of millions of Jews killed by the Germans during World War II: US and British troops found horrible piles of corpses in the west German camps they captured in 1945 (e.g. Dachau and Belsen); there are no longer large communities of Jews in Poland; and historians generally support the legend.

During both world wars Germany was forced to fight typhus, carried by lice in the constant traffic with the east. That is why all accounts of entry into the German concentration camps speak of shaving of hair and showering and other delousing procedures, such as treatment of quarters with the pesticide Zyklon. That was also the main reason for a high death rate in the camps, and the crematoria that existed in all.

(Source: http://pubweb.acns.nwu.edu/~abutz/di/intro.html)

The pupils simply added this text to the collection, from which their class colleagues were later to work on extracting and summarising information. It was not until I sat with the group and we did a careful shared reading of this text that they noticed that it was radically at odds with the other texts they had collected on this subject.

I should point out that this group of pupils were all operating at average or above-average levels in their literacy. They were all very able to discuss texts in terms of their structural features, to explain the different uses of connective words and phrases within texts, to talk knowledgeably about tense use, active and passive sentences, and vocabulary choice. They had been taught well according to the Literacy Framework. But this ability had only taken them so far. Their need, when faced with texts like the above, was to ask critical questions such as: 'What is the evidence for the claims this text makes?'; 'What is the author trying to convince me of?'; 'How do I know whether to believe this or not?'.

Asking questions such as these involves the operation of critical literacy, an ability which is probably even more essential today than it has ever been. We are all, adults and children alike, constantly bombarded with text which tries, sometimes blatantly and sometimes extraordinarily subtly, to persuade us to a certain viewpoint or action. Fully literate people are aware of such persuasion and know how, or whether, to resist it. Critical literacy is a crucial skill for surviving in the information-dense twenty-first century.

What is critical literacy?

Of course, critical literacy is not an entirely new concept and there have been a number of definitions of what it involves. Critical literacy is rather like a chameleon, changing from context to context. It is known in different parts of the world as: critical language awareness, critical social literacy, critically aware literacy etc. Nevertheless, there are at least four common threads to the different approaches to critical literacy that can give us a useful starting point for identifying its key characteristics.

First, critical literacy rests on an assumption that language education can make a difference in children's lives, particularly those children who fall outside what we call the 'mainstream'. Being literate in a 'basic' sense is not enough on its own to bring about large-scale changes in people's everyday lives. Yet teachers who value critical literacy will tend to have a stake in social change – even small change – and will encourage their pupils to investigate, question and even challenge relationships between language and social practices that advantage particular social groups over others.

Secondly, critical literacy approaches assume that the meanings of words and texts (which can be verbal, digital, printed, moving or pictorial) cannot be separated from the cultural and social practices in which, and by which, they are constructed. The way that we use language to read, write, view, speak and listen is never neutral or value-free. Even activities as seemingly benign as reading a picture book to young children are culturally and politically complex. We select texts we deem to be appropriate and thereby present a culture. Although not the only possible culture, what we have selected becomes naturalised as 'the way things are, or ought to be', potentially excluding children who belong to and identify with different cultures.

Thirdly, critical literacy is about analysing and evaluating something. Ira Shor (1992: 32), for example, emphasises the key roles of analysis and critique in critical literacy. For him, critical literacy is:

> analytic habits of thinking, reading, writing, speaking, or discussing which go beneath surface impressions, traditional myths, mere opinions, and routine clichés; understanding the social contexts

and consequences of any subject matter; discovering the deep meaning of any event, text, technique, process, object, statement, image, or situation; applying that meaning to your own context.

Analysing and evaluating texts goes beyond simply recognising that they are not value-free to looking at how some texts fit more easily with the experiences of particular groups of readers and writers and their views of the world.

Fourthly, some idea of what it means to be socially aware and active citizens runs through most of the writing about critical literacy. Chris Searle (1998), for example, discusses developing what he calls 'imaginative empathy' in his pupils. He uses a range of texts to encourage them to imagine themselves in the lives of others and to write poetry and prose from these different viewpoints. The outcomes include books of professionally produced poetry that try to challenge the racial and class tensions that characterise their schools and communities. Seen this way, critical literacy is about transforming taken-for-granted social and language practices or assumptions for the good of as many people as possible (Freire 1972).

How can we teach critical literacy?

There are a number of teaching approaches and strategies that can be used to develop critical literacy in primary pupils. I will group these into four major categories. These are:

- textual analysis;
- text clustering;
- texts for social action; and
- critical writing.

Textual analysis

Here is an extract from a book found on the library shelf of a Warwickshire primary school. The book is *History Can Be Fun* by Munro Leaf. Although this book was originally first published in 1950 (in the US), the 1976 British edition is very attractively illustrated and appealingly presented. It was clearly being used in this primary school.

> ...now that you've read this far you'll know what generally happened as soon as a new country was discovered. Two things, first, other nations came along and tried to get a share, second, the native people, like the Indians and 'red' Indians, found themselves being ruled by white men. With Australia and New Zealand things were better. No other European nation tried to take them, and in Australia there were only a very few black people so that colonists did not have to lead armies against them. In New Zealand there were splendid native people called Maoris and they fought against the British at first. But now the Maoris and the settlers who have come from Britain live peacefully side by side and there are Maori members of the New Zealand Parliament.

Passages like this are not uncommon in school history books, especially those written before the beginning of the 1970s, and can be a useful source of textual analysis practice for primary pupils.

Key points in this text to draw to pupils' attention are:

- the suggestion that countries were unknown before Europeans set foot there: '...as soon as a *new country was discovered* ...';

- the way the text provides the opinions or viewpoint of one group only: 'With Australia and New Zealand *things were better*'. Better for whom?;

- the way it minimises the damage and distress caused by colonisation to indigenous peoples: '...the Indians and "red" Indians *found themselves being ruled* by white men'. "But now the Maoris and the settlers ...*live peacefully side by side...*'.

This sort of textual analysis can be guided by asking the pupils to go fairly systematically through a list of questions such as the following:

- What is the subject or topic of this text?

- Why might the author have written it?

- Who is it written for? How do you know?

- What values does the author assume the reader holds? How do you know?

- What knowledge does the reader need to bring to the text in order to understand it?

- Who would feel 'left out' in this text and why? Who would feel that the claims made in the text clash with their own values, beliefs or experiences?

- How is the reader 'positioned' in relation to the author (e.g. as a friend, as an opponent, as someone who needs to be persuaded, as invisible, as someone who agrees with the author's views)?

Another approach to giving pupils a systematic way of analysing texts can be to use a checklist. One such checklist, developed particularly for use in evaluating websites, is the CARS Checklist (Figure 8.1), based around a number of criteria which can be used to judge the quality of information in texts. These criteria are summarised as CARS – Credibility, Accuracy, Reasonableness, Support. Few texts will meet every criterion in the list, but in learning to apply these criteria, pupils will significantly sharpen their critical faculties regarding textual information.

Further information about each of these criteria is given below.

Credibility

Because people have always made important decisions based on information, evidence of authenticity and reliability – credibility – has always been important. If we read a newspaper article saying that the area where we live will experience major flooding in the next few weeks, it is important to know whether or not to believe the information. Some questions to ask would include:

- What makes this text believable (or not)?

- How does the author know this information?

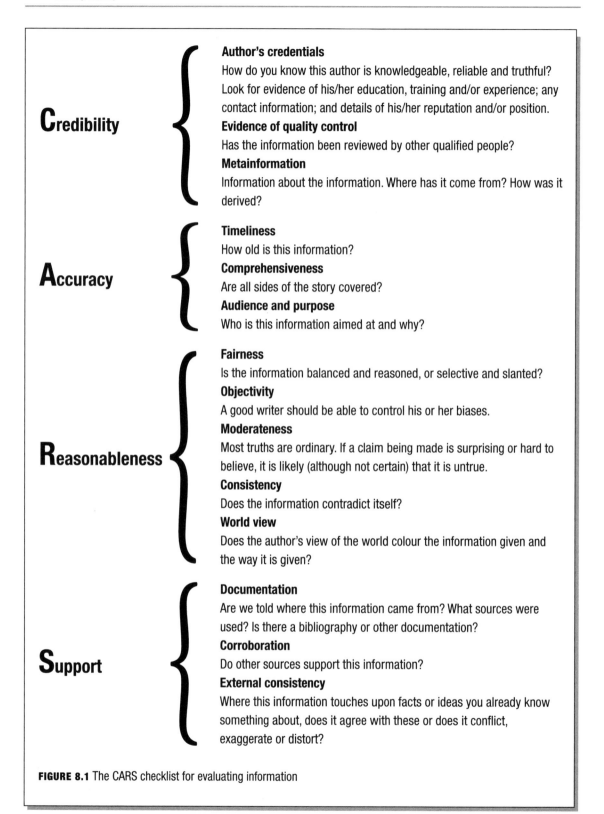

Credibility {

Author's credentials
How do you know this author is knowledgeable, reliable and truthful? Look for evidence of his/her education, training and/or experience; any contact information; and details of his/her reputation and/or position.
Evidence of quality control
Has the information been reviewed by other qualified people?
Metainformation
Information about the information. Where has it come from? How was it derived?

Accuracy {

Timeliness
How old is this information?
Comprehensiveness
Are all sides of the story covered?
Audience and purpose
Who is this information aimed at and why?

Reasonableness {

Fairness
Is the information balanced and reasoned, or selective and slanted?
Objectivity
A good writer should be able to control his or her biases.
Moderateness
Most truths are ordinary. If a claim being made is surprising or hard to believe, it is likely (although not certain) that it is untrue.
Consistency
Does the information contradict itself?
World view
Does the author's view of the world colour the information given and the way it is given?

Support {

Documentation
Are we told where this information came from? What sources were used? Is there a bibliography or other documentation?
Corroboration
Do other sources support this information?
External consistency
Where this information touches upon facts or ideas you already know something about, does it agree with these or does it conflict, exaggerate or distort?

FIGURE 8.1 The CARS checklist for evaluating information

There are several tests which can be applied to a text to help judge how credible it will be:

Author's credentials

The author or text of the information should show some evidence of being knowledgeable, reliable and truthful. Here are some clues:

- The author's education, training and/or experience is in an area relevant to the information. Look for biographical details, the author's title or position of employment.
- The author provides contact information (email or postal address, phone number).
- The author has a sound reputation or previous publications to his credit.

Evidence of quality control

Most information texts should pass through a review process, where several readers examine and approve the content before it is published. Statements issued in the name of an organisation have almost always been seen and approved by several people.

Indicators of lack of credibility

You can sometimes tell by the tone, style or competence of the writing whether or not the information is suspect. Here are a few clues:

- anonymity;
- lack of quality control;
- negative reviews;
- bad grammar or misspelled words; this suggests carelessness or ignorance, neither of which puts the writer in a favourable light.

Accuracy

The aim of the accuracy test is to ensure that the information is actually correct: up-to-date, factual, detailed, exact and comprehensive. For example, even though a very credible writer said something that was correct 20 years ago, it may not be correct today. Similarly, a reputable text might be giving up-to-date information, but the information may be only partial and may not give the full story. Here are some things to bear in mind when judging accuracy:

Timeliness

Some texts are timeless, like classic novels and stories, but others have a limited useful life because of advances in knowledge, and some are outdated very quickly (like texts about computers). We must, therefore, be careful to note when information was created and then decide whether it is still of value.

Comprehensiveness

Any text that presents conclusions, or that claims to give a full picture, should try to be complete, i.e. comprehensive. Some people argue that writers should be sure that they have 'complete' information before producing a text. But there is so much information available now that completeness is probably impossible. Nobody can read every single piece of research on a subject. So no single piece of information will give the complete story. That is why it is a good idea to get into the habit of consulting more than one text.

On the other hand, an information text that deliberately leaves out important facts, or alternatives, may be misleading or intentionally deceptive.

Indicators of a lack of accuracy

There are several indicators that may mean the text is inaccurate, either in whole or in part:

- no date on the document;
- vague or sweeping generalisations;
- old date on information known to change rapidly;
- very one-sided view that does not acknowledge opposing views or respond to them.

Reasonableness

The test of reasonableness involves examining the information for fairness, objectivity and moderateness.

Fairness

Fairness includes offering a balanced, reasoned argument, not selected or slanted. Even claims made by the text's opponents should be presented in an accurate manner. Pretending that the opponent has wild, irrational ideas or arguments that nobody could possibly accept is not usually reasonable.

A good information text will also have a calm, reasoned tone, arguing or presenting material thoughtfully, without attempting to get the reader worked up emotionally.

Objectivity

It is difficult for writers to be completely objective, but a good text should not be obviously biased. One of the biggest hindrances to objectivity is conflict of interest. Sometimes the author of a text will benefit in some way if that text can get the reader to accept certain information as the truth.

Moderateness

If a text makes a claim that is surprising or hard to believe, the reader needs to demand more evidence than might be required for a lesser claim. Is the information believable? Does it make sense?

Indicators of a lack of reasonableness

Some clues to a lack of reasonableness are:

- intemperate language ('these stupid people'; 'those who believe differently are obviously deranged');

- overclaims ('Thousands of children are murdered every day in the United Kingdom');
- sweeping statements ('This is the most important idea ever suggested!');
- conflict of interest ('Welcome to the United Tobacco Company Home Page. To read our report, "Cigarettes Make You Live Longer", click here').

Support

The area of support is concerned with the corroboration of the information in a text. Much information comes from other texts, and making reference to these will strengthen the credibility of the text. Support can be given in a number of ways:

Bibliography

- Where did this information come from?
- What texts did the author use?
- Are these listed?

It is especially important for figures to be documented. Otherwise, the author might just be making up the numbers.

Corroboration

See if other texts support this text. If an argument is sound, there will probably be a number of people who agree with it. It is a good idea to triangulate information, that is find at least three texts that agree. If other texts do not agree, further research into the range of opinion or disagreement is needed.

Indicators of a lack of support

Readers should be careful when a text shows problems like these:

- numbers or statistics are presented without an identified source for them;
- you cannot find any other texts that present the same information or acknowledge that the same information exists.

Text clustering

Text clustering refers to the activity of deliberately confronting pupils with texts that obviously contradict each other. The task of the pupils is to use whatever evidence they can find to try to make judgements about where the truth actually lies. Sometimes these judgements are relatively easy to make.

Some Year 5 pupils were recently investigating the planets and found the following conflicting information about Saturn.

1. From the BBC News website (http://news.bbc.co.uk/1/hi/sci/tech/992494.stm) (page dated Thursday, 26 October 2000):

Four new moons found circling Saturn

By BBC News online science editor Dr David Whitehouse

Saturn has become the planet with the greatest number of known moons, 22, following the discovery of four new satellites around it. The four, faint bodies were detected during the past few months by several telescopes around the world. Further studies in the next few months will establish the satellites' precise orbits around the ringed planet.

2. From the Ananova website (http://www.ananova.com/news/story/sm_349369.html) (page dated Wednesday, 11 July 2001):

New moons discovered around Saturn

Astronomers have discovered 12 new moons around Saturn, bringing the planet's tally to 30 – the largest satellite family in the Solar System. The new moons are small, measuring between 6 and 30 kilometres in diameter, and move in irregular, tilted orbits. They fall into several clusters, leading scientists to conclude that they are the remnants of larger moons fragmented by collisions. The moons probably began life as wandering bodies that were captured by Saturn's gravity.

The children were puzzled about how many moons Saturn actually has, and how to reconcile this conflicting information about when these moons were discovered. Further investigation revealed a third text.

3. From the Science Line website (http://www.sciencenet.org.uk/database/phys/astronomy/solarsystem/Jupiter/p00958b.html) (undated page)

Satellites orbiting Saturn [date discovered in brackets]

Pan (1990); Atlas (1980); Prometheus (1980); Janus (1966); Enceladus (1789); Tethys (1684); Telesto (1980); Pandora (1980); Epimetheus (1966); Mimas (1789); Calypso (1980); Dione (1684); Helene (1980); Rhea (1672); Titan (1655); Hyperion (1848); Iapetus (1671); Phoebe (1898).

The pupils' conclusion (with teacher help) was that the number of moons thought to orbit Saturn depended upon the date that particular moons had been discovered. Therefore, it was important when reading information like this to pay particular attention to the date the information was written.

Another longer and more complex activity along these lines is described in the next section. The activity is given in the form of two literacy hour lesson plans, although it obviously could be carried out in a range of different ways.

Unit of work title: Is spinach good for you?

Lesson 1

> *Whole class activity (20 minutes):*
> Show the class the Ediets web page entitled 'Iron – the Not-so-Wimpy Nutrient!' (http://www.edietsuk.co.uk/news/article.cfm/article_id,1541). The page relates to the topic of 'Is eating spinach good for you?' Read the text together and discuss its meaning. (The text below is only a selection from that on the web page.)

Iron – the Not-so-Wimpy Nutrient!

Aileen McGloin

Anyone who grew up watching Popeye eating mounds of spinach knows that iron is one of the essential nutrients. Most people also think that spinach is a pretty good source of this nutrient as a result of this popular cartoon. The truth is that early in this century, when scientists were testing for the iron content of spinach, long before automated printers, they wrote down the wrong results. Someone put the decimal point in the wrong place and for a long time people believed that spinach contained ten times more iron than it really did. Spinach does contain some iron, but it isn't the best source. Red meat is the best source, so maybe Wimpy, with his love of hamburgers, should have been the one fighting Bluto for the love of Olive Oyle! Iron is also found in oily fish, the dark meat of chicken and turkey and in some nuts, seeds, dried fruits, dark green vegetables and fortified breakfast cereals.

Introduce the *For and Against Grid* (Figure 8.2). Ideally, you should use an enlarged version of this grid, which can easily be seen by the whole class. With the aid of the pupils, enter some points for and against the central question on the grid. Make sure you write 'Ediets' against each point and explain how important it is to record the source of arguments.

Spend a little time discussing with the class whether the information given on this page is likely to be true or not. You might show them the Ediets home page to try to get a sense of the motivation of this group for giving this information. They want people to pay to use the service they offer, but there seems no obvious reason why they should be biased about spinach. You might also get the pupils to question the fact that no corroboratory evidence is given for the decimal point mistake. This could itself be a myth.

> *Group activity (30 minutes):*
> Pupils should work in groups to repeat the above activity using other web pages and building up a list of for and against points on their copies of the grid. Web pages suitable for this are listed below:

Is spinach good for you?

Points for	Points against

Remember to include the source of your information

FIGURE 8.2 The for and against grid

http://www.botanical.com/botanical/mgmh/s/spinac80.html
This looks at first sight to be highly scientific and thus, perhaps, more credible, but pupils should be able to spot that the information given here is dated. They are actually warned about this on the most recent version of this web page.

http://www.wholehealthmd.com/refshelf/foods_view/1,1523,35,00.html
This seems to be both scientific and up to date, and provides a number of points in support of the idea that spinach is good for you. However, if pupils go to the home page of this website they will find the statement that the originator of the site, WholeHealthMD.com, 'is dedicated to providing the best in complementary and alternative medicine', that is they are not a mainstream medical company. Pupils could debate whether this makes the information they give more or less reliable.

http://www.vrg.org/nutrition/iron.htm

This page looks very scientific, with a number of impressive tables of information. Table 2, in particular, seems to demonstrate that spinach is a much richer source of iron than any meat product, containing four times as much iron as sirloin steak. Pupils should think carefully, however, about what this table means. The proportions of iron are given as milligrams per 100 calories. Clearly, 100 calories worth of spinach takes up a good deal more space than 100 calories worth of steak, so the table is somewhat misleading. They should follow this up by looking at the originators of this web page, The Vegetarian Resource Group, and ask the question about how unbiased a presentation this is likely to be.

http://www.beefinfo.org/bh_iron.cfm

This web page advances the opposite opinion to the previous one, giving a convincing-sounding argument about two types of iron, of which only one is really good for you – the iron that is found in meat rather than in spinach. Again pupils need to look at the originators of this page, the Beef Information Centre, which is described as 'a division of the Canadian Cattlemen's Association', that is a group with a vested interest in selling beef.

Plenary activity (10 minutes):
Review the work of the groups so far and discuss their conclusions regarding the likely accuracy of the websites they have used.

Lesson 2

Whole-class activity (20 minutes):
Introduce the class to the blank writing frame (Figure 8.3) (preferably an enlarged version or a transparency). Take the class through this, getting suggestions about how it might be completed, modelling the writing of several sections, and also demonstrating how to record details of the sources of the points being made.

Group activity (25 minutes):
Pupils should now work in groups or individually to complete their own versions of the writing frame, using points they have earlier noted on their grids. They should record the sources of the points they make.

Plenary activity (15 minutes):
Ask groups or individuals to present the writing they have completed so far. Discuss the merits of the points made and whether the writers have treated them sufficiently fairly or critically.

Is spinach good for you?

There are contrasting views about this issue. There is some evidence to suggest that

but other evidence suggests that

One piece of evidence that suggests spinach is good for you is that

Along the same lines, it also seems that

Furthermore

However, it is also necessary to consider the following points. First,

It is also possible that

It can also be seen that

Taking all these points into consideration it would seem that

I therefore conclude that

FIGURE 8.3 A discussion writing frame

Follow-up activity:
Pupils can complete their writing using the notes they have made on their grids. If they have internet access at home, they could also be asked to collect some further information about the nutritional value of spinach and, in particular, research whether the Popeye myth is simply due to a typing error.

Other activities

Other sources of material for text-clustering activities include:

Newspaper reports

Take a current event about which there will be reports in several daily newspapers. Collect the reports on this event in four or five newspapers, making sure you include a range of tabloids, broadsheets etc. Use extracts from some of these reports for shared reading. As you read, demonstrate to the class the kinds of questions you might ask yourself to judge the credibility and accuracy of each report. Ask groups of pupils to compare pairs of reports and to list the questions they have about items which might seem to conflict. Bring the class together to discuss what they have found. Draw their attention to (among other things):

- **Selective quoting.** Newspaper reporters will all get their original information from the same speech by a person involved in the event, or the same press release. Why do they often quote slightly differently, or not quote at all?
- **Use of descriptors.** Look at the use of adjectives and adverbs in reports. Often these are chosen to give an impression to the reader. What impression, and why does the newspaper want to give it?
- **Order in which the event is reported.** Newspaper editors know that the average reader only ever reads the first couple of paragraphs of any given report. What information do they choose to go in these first paragraphs, and what is left until later? Why might they plan things this way?

Everyday texts

Ask pupils to collect examples of texts they see around their homes for comparison in school sessions. Advertisements, brochures and leaflets are all good sources of such texts. Get the pupils to look carefully at how different texts, which, apparently, are doing similar jobs, are written and structured differently.

As an example of this kind of activity, look at the three texts given in Figures 8.4, 8.5 and 8.6. They were each found in a hotel room.

Questions to get pupils to ask about these texts include:

- Two of the texts talk about 'our environment', and one says 'the environment'. What difference does this make to the way the reader responds?
- Two texts ask for the reader's help: 'Help us to help our environment'. One text simply tells us what to do. Again, what effect does this have on the reader?
- Notice the use of 'by kindly considering using these bathroom towels a second time' in the Best Western notice. This is a very gentle way of asking readers to do something. Compare it with the more direct language of the other two texts.
- Why does the Menzies Hotel notice only mention towels *after* it has told the reader what the hotel has done to help the environment?
- Notice that none of these notices mentions the fact that the less washing of guests' towels the hotel has to do, the smaller its laundry bill will be.

Help Us to Help Our Environment

Environmental care is often a matter of taking little steps
which reduce the demands on the earth's natural resources.
Help us to do this by kindly considering using
the bathroom towels a second time.

Place your towels on the towel rail to USE THEM AGAIN

Place your towels in the bath or shower to CHANGE THEM

FIGURE 8.4 Hotel notice 1

Royal Hotel
KIRKWALL

In the interests of the environment

Imagine just how many towels are
unnecessarily washed each day in all the
hotels throughout the world.

The truckloads of washing powder used,
the reservoirs of water needed and the
energy consumed to wash and dry them.

**Towels placed in the bath/shower
means please exchange**

**Towels replaced on the towel rail
means I will use again**

Thank you for your co-operation

FIGURE 8.5 Hotel notice 2

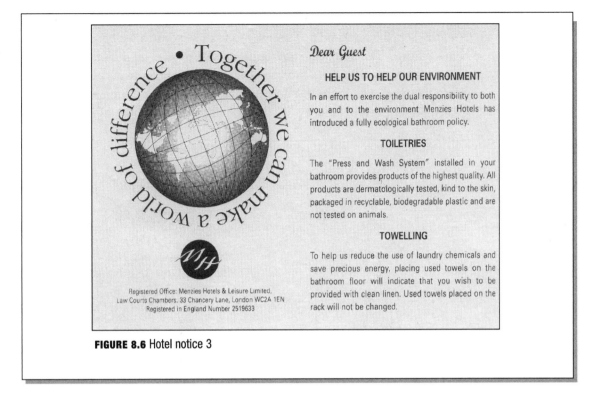

FIGURE 8.6 Hotel notice 3

Stories

Younger children will enjoy comparing different versions of well-known fairy stories and discussing how these make them feel. One class of six-year-olds were read a version of the story (taken from Andrew Lang's *Blue Fairy Book*, first published in 1899), which ends with both Red Riding Hood and the grandmother being eaten by the wolf. This caused great discussion as the children compared other versions they knew. One little boy spent a good ten minutes trying to find what he insisted must be a page missing from the story (the bit where the woodcutter comes to rescue Red Riding Hood) and was only persuaded that there was no missing page by looking at the page numbers in the book.

Texts for social action

We have always known the importance of authentic literacy experiences for children's literacy development. When pupils are given opportunities to engage in purposeful and 'urgent' reading and writing, they begin to see the point of literacy and of the learning and practising the skills of literacy. Yet it has always been extremely difficult to provide many pupils with these authentic literacy experiences. In writing, for example, the accepted wisdom is that providing pupils with real audiences will improve their writing skills. Few children, however, experience writing for an audience other than their teachers. Even when they are told that the audience is elsewhere, they usually know that, in fact, the writing will not be sent to that 'else-where' but will be read and judged by their teacher.

If we wish our pupils to experience the power of literacy to influence people, then we need at some point to allow them the time and opportunity to use literacy in a really socially active way. Sometimes this requires planning. One teacher in north Devon used the sad occasion of a serious traffic accident outside the school to teach her pupils how to write persuasive letters. Letters were sent to many people, including local councillors and the Prime Minister. The letter sent to the local MP is given in Figure 8.7.

> 59 Sowden park
> forches
> Barnstaple
> devon
> Ex328ef
> 17\11\95
>
> Dear Nick Harvey,
> Although not every body would agree, I want to argue that: Adult's should not drink and drive.
> I have several reason's for arguing for this point of veiw, my first reason is: Drunk people could have a hangover and feel ill but even more they lose concentration and crash! into a child or adult or mabee both. A further reason is:
> We have enough drunk driver's here in Barnstaple, I hate thinking about this matter.
> furthermore I think this is stupid to do nothing about this. therefore although some argue that I am wrong I think I have shown that (drinking and driving kills!
> Your's Sincerely Christopher Tomlin

FIGURE 8.7 A letter to an MP

At other times the teacher needs to be able to step back and allow pupils the space to engage in this socially active literacy. An example of this is the teacher in Southampton whose school had been the subject of a local newspaper investigation into the quality of school dinners. The pupils were outraged by the report when it appeared and demanded to be allowed to write to the reporter responsible, one Lucy Hines. One of the letters she received is given in Figure 8.8.

Harefield Middle School
Yeovil Chase
Harefield
Southampton
SO2 5NZ

1/12/95

Dear Sir or Madam,

You are very deceitful, just trying to do a good report, eh? Well I totally disagree with what that Lucy Hines has reported. How COULD she say that the dinner ladies glare down at you and make you eat all your dinner up? If you don't want it, you don't have to eat it. We have the best dinner ladies any school could ever wish for. Mrs Self and her dinner ladies cook the dinners as best they can. And Lucy said that the peas are mushy. Well of course they're mushy, thats why they're called MUSHY PEAS! As for soggy carrots, well they were tinned and grated carrots. If Lucy didn't like them she shouldn't have taken them. And how DARE she lie and say we had lumpy custard and gravy? We didn't even have any of them! In fact, here's the menu:

DINNER: Spaghetti Bolognaise, Fish, Burgers, Peas, Carrots, Sweet Corn, Salad, Beetroot, Coleslaw.
PUDDING: Cream Bun, Biscuits, Fruit, Yoghurt, Fruit Juice.

Healthy or what? Well that sly, dopey Lucy Hines should lose her job as far as Harefield Middle School and I are concerned. We are feeling extremely cross about it and most defiant.

Yours Sincerely,

Sophie Thomson

FIGURE 8.8 A letter to a newspaper

Unfortunately the school have no record of having received a reply from Lucy Hines or the newspaper, which would have been even more effective in allowing these pupils to see the value of socially active literacy.

Critical writing

Thinking about the ways in which literacy can be an authentic social activity in schools inevitably leads us into thinking about writing. Children more obviously impact upon their social worlds when they write. Writing is a social activity; there is little point in doing it unless someone else will read the outcome.

Another aspect to writing, however, which bears strongly upon the issue of critical literacy, is the contention that in learning to write in order to deliberately influence and persuade other people, children are at the same time learning the 'tricks' of writing persuasively, so that when they read others' persuasive text they are more able to recognise the tricks and techniques being employed against them. Learning to write effectively teaches children to read more effectively.

If this argument is correct, then one of the most important teaching strategies for developing critical reading is to teach persuasive writing explicitly. How can this be done?

A model outlined in an earlier chapter suggests a number of steps in the explicit teaching of writing. You can:

1. provide models of writing and focus pupils' attention on how these work;
2. demonstrate writing processes;
3. participate in writing tasks alongside pupils; and
4. scaffold pupils in producing writing.

These steps can be summarised in the acronym IDES: Immersion; Deconstruction; Exemplification; Scaffolding.

Immersion

Just as a crucial factor in babies learning to talk is to immerse them in spoken language, so pupils learning to write persuasively need to be immersed in examples of persuasive writing. We have always had a tendency to surround pupils with texts we perceive to be neutral, i.e. that simply give them information rather than try to persuade them to a particular point of view. There are good reasons for this, of course. Teachers do not want to be accused of trying to influence children through the texts they use, and persuasive texts, by their very nature, can be quite controversial.

Unless pupils are confronted regularly with such persuasive and controversial texts and, *crucially*, taught to examine these texts critically, they run a greater risk of being unconsciously influenced by such texts when they encounter them outside the classroom environment.

The *National Literacy Strategy Framework for Teaching* sets the target that in Year 4, term 3 pupils should be taught:

16. to read, compare and evaluate examples of arguments and discussions, e.g. letters to press, articles, discussion of issues in books, e.g. environment, animal welfare;

17. how arguments are presented, e.g. ordering points to link them together so that one follows from another; how statistics, graphs etc. can be used to support arguments;

18. from examples of persuasive writing, to investigate how style and vocabulary are used to convince the intended reader;

19. to evaluate advertisements for their impact, appeal and honesty, focusing in particular on how information about the product is presented: exaggerated claims, tactics for grabbing attention, linguistic devices, e.g. puns, jingles, alliteration, invented words;

These targets might well be thought too late, as children will be exposed to persuasive texts long before they are eight years old and need to know how to react. But they cannot be met without bringing into the classroom persuasive texts of all kinds for children to read and study.

Deconstruction

Of course, it is not simply by having persuasive texts available that pupils will learn how they work and how to resist them. They need to engage in deconstruction of these texts; that is to explore how the texts are structured and how their style and choice of words makes them persuasive. One of the most powerful teaching approaches to this is shared reading. By closely examining a text together, a great many textual tricks and techniques can be learnt. As an example of this, the text given in Figure 8.9 might be used with Year 5 or 6 pupils.

One way of using this text is to begin by reading it aloud to the class. Each pupil should have in front of them a copy of the chart in Figure 8.10. Ask them to tick the phrases as they hear them. You may need to read the text a couple of times.

Then introduce the class to the analysis chart given in Figure 8.11. The pupils may need talking through this a section at a time, or some might be able to work on it as part of a group. You will need a great deal of plenary work on this chart to ensure that pupils understand the text features they have been exploring.

Exemplification

Exemplification simply means the teacher demonstrating how to write persuasive texts, and is the essence of shared writing. Remember that the point of shared writing is not so much the pupils *watching* the teacher write but *hearing* the teacher think aloud as he/she explains the processes involved in the composition. Shared writing, whether it involves a demonstration of composition by the teacher, the teacher scribing what the pupils compose or supporting their composition with suggestions of his/her own, has four major purposes:

1. it models for children how writers think, making visible the otherwise hidden mental processes that make up writing;

2. it provides a demonstration of how to compose, a process that can seem mysterious to novice writers;

3. it provides an active demonstration of the full writing process, including

- selecting or clarifying the writing task;
- collecting and connecting information;
- gathering ideas and researching;
- planning;
- transcribing, reading and revising;
- doing final editing and proofreading;
- getting feedback on what has been written; and

4. it shows that writing needs to be purposeful and written with readers in mind.

Meat is murder

Although not everyone would agree with me, I want to argue that eating meat is unhealthy, unethical and unnecessary. Therefore we should not do it.

My first reason for arguing this way is that meat-eaters are generally not as healthy as vegetarians. Some studies, for example, have found that people who ate meat were more likely to develop cancer than people who did not. Meat-eaters are also more likely to die of heart attacks. If it causes such a risk to your health, why on earth would you want to eat meat?

A further reason that eating meat is wrong is that it causes such cruelty. For instance, animals being taken to the abattoir often travel in terrible conditions, and when they arrive they are treated horrifically. How would you feel if you had to travel hundreds of miles packed tightly in a lorry with no food or water?

Furthermore, I strongly believe that eating meat is totally unnecessary. Some studies have shown, for instance, that we can get 100% (yes 100%!) of our food requirements from vegetables, dairy products such as milk and cheese, and pulses (beans and lentils). Meat, in fact, provides us with far more calories, protein and fat than we actually need. Therefore, why would you want to eat meat?

Although some people would argue that eating meat is natural, my conviction is that eating meat is wrong. It is bad for our health, bad for the animals and totally unnecessary. I urge you to consider these facts.

I think I have given plenty of reasons why we should ban the eating of meat. Therefore let's ban it now. Meat is murder! We don't need it! It's bad for us. It should be banned.

FIGURE 8.9 A persuasive text

Listen to the piece of persuasive writing and tick the following words and phrases as you hear them:

I want to argue that	
My first reason	
For example	
A further reason	
For instance	
Furthermore	
I strongly believe	
How would you feel	
Why would you	
I urge you	
It should be	

FIGURE 8.10 A listening frame

Scaffolding

The teaching model which begins with teacher demonstration has as its end point the pupils engaging independently in the activity being demonstrated. Shared writing should lead to pupils writing independently using similar knowledge and skills to those which have been demonstrated to them. But the jump from teacher demonstration to pupil independence is not usually a rapid or a simple one. Especially in writing, learners need support as they begin to work independently, in our case on producing persuasive writing. Such support can take a number of forms:

Collaborative writing, in which pupils work together, either with or without a teacher, to compose a piece of persuasive writing, can offer hesitant writers a context in which to extend their skills. Here, the support comes from other writers who may or may not be more expert at the particular writing task.

Supported writing, in which pupils write following the guidance of a prompt sheet such as that given in Figure 5.2, Chapter 5, may offer a way of jogging their memories about the key features of the writing they are attempting.

Framed writing offers more extensive support for writing by guiding pupils in the structure of the text they are composing, and the use of key connective phrases. An example of a persuasive writing frame is given in Figure 8.12, but more can be found in Lewis and Wray (1997).

1. Structure

The piece is organised into sections. Complete the following table:

Section	What is it doing?	How many paragraphs?
Section 1	Introduces the argument	1
Section 2	Makes the first point. Gives some examples. Finishes with a question.	
Section 3		
Section 4		
Section 5		

2. Type of language

Type of language	Example	Your example from the text
emotive	'I strongly believe that …'	
factual	'We can get 100% of our food requirements …'	

3. Connective words

Type of connective	Example	Your example
additive	furthermore	
logical	therefore	

4. Language devices

Language device	Example	Your example
Pattern of three	unhealthy, unethical and unnecessary	
Alliteration	meat is murder	
Rhetorical question	Why on earth would you want to eat meat?	
Involving the audience	I urge you to …	

FIGURE 8.11 Analysing persuasive writing

Although not everybody would agree, I want to argue that

I have several reasons for arguing for this point of view. My first reason is

A further reason is

Furthermore,

Therefore, although some people argue that

I think I have shown that

FIGURE 8.12 A persuasive writing frame

Conclusion

I have tried to suggest in this chapter that critical literacy is not a luxury that can wait until pupils have mastered the basics of reading and writing; rather, it should inform our teaching of literacy from the very beginning. At root it is about recognising, and helping our pupils to recognise, that texts do not simply appear – they are written by someone. In the process of that writing, the author of the text, whether an individual or a group of individuals, had to make decisions about which meanings were represented in the text and how they would be represented. Critical literacy refers to the awareness of the reader that this decision-making process has occurred, and will have affected the meanings it is possible for the reader to construct from the text.

The chapter has suggested a number of ways of building a critical literacy perspective into literacy teaching. The strategies it discusses are not to be used exclusively in lessons called 'literacy', but have relevance right across the curriculum. Critical literacy should be a key component of the teaching of any subject.

CHAPTER

Reading electronic texts

Introduction: expanding literacy

I recently bought a new laptop computer and, being heavily influenced by advertisements, acquired an example of what has become known as a Tablet PC. This is different from normal laptops in two main ways: its screen can flip over onto the top of its keyboard, making it a little like a chunky A4 writing pad but with a surface of screen rather than paper; and it comes supplied with a special pen with which I can write on the screen, which then either treats my handwriting as a picture or converts it to computer text. As a machine, it is liberating. I can use it to handwrite notes in meetings, which are then automatically converted to typed text. I have a large collection of electronic books, any of which I can read easily on the tablet screen, so on long train or plane journeys it is like carrying 100 books with me to select my reading from. (The only problem with this is that the battery life is only about three hours, but in some modern trains you can actually plug the laptop into a mains socket.)

One of the most exciting features of my new computer is that it came complete with a folder entitled 'My Magazines'. Inside this were electronic copies of a range of magazines (e.g. *Newsweek*, *Time*, *Personal Computer World*, *New Statesman*), all of which look exactly like their printed versions with a few crucial differences:

- When I open one of these magazines, I get a double-page spread sideways on my A4 screen. This is at a good enough resolution for me to skim the page contents and, if I see an article or picture I want to look at in more detail, I touch it with the special pen and the view instantly zooms in so that I can read both text and pictures easily. If I touch it again it zooms back out.

- If I find an article I am particularly interested in I can select the whole of it with the pen and then copy it to a blank page. I can do this with several pieces, thus ending up with my own personal magazine of articles I really do want to read.

- I can use the pen to handwrite onto the magazine, making annotations easy. The touch of a button, however, makes these annotations disappear. (The touch of another button makes them return should I decide I erased them too quickly.)

- If I come across a technical word or phrase I am not too sure about, in most cases just hovering my pen above it makes a small window appear containing a definition.

- Hovering the pen over other words, phrases, pictures and captions brings up small windows containing lists of other places in the magazine to which I can instantly jump. For example, a piece about building a computer tells me that I need to include a graphics card. Holding my pen above the words 'graphics card' produces the suggestion that if I want to read more about different kinds of graphic cards I can go to another article in the magazine, and touching this text takes me to the article instantly. When I have finished reading about graphics cards I can jump back instantly to where I was originally.

Just a short period of experience with My Magazines convinces me that I am engaged here in a completely different kind of reading. It is a reading in which I am in control of the order and sequence of text I encounter and in which I can actively contribute to creating the text I read. It is also a reading in which it is hard to relax since I have to make decisions all the time.

Traditionally, literacy has been defined simply as the condition of being able to read and write, and for most people this definition is adequate. However, it is becoming increasingly apparent that we need to expand our definition of literacy to include the reading and writing not only of printed texts but also of electronic texts. Until recently, teachers could safely confine reading and writing activities to printed materials. Increasingly, however, reading and writing can be done electronically with the aid of a computer. Computers are being used to create and revise texts, to send and receive mail electronically, to present texts of all kinds on screen instead of in printed books, and to access large databases of texts. Electronic texts are becoming more prevalent as computers become an integral part of everyday experiences such as working, shopping, travelling and studying.

Clearly, teachers need to include electronic forms of reading and writing in the literacy experiences they offer to their pupils. This creates two main issues for consideration, both of which I will explore in this and the following chapter:

1. How are electronic texts different from printed texts?
2. How can learners be prepared to read and write electronically?

The characteristics of electronic texts

In this section I will briefly discuss four fundamental differences between printed and electronic texts. I try here to go beyond the mere surface differences between the two media. A screen looks different from a page, but that in itself need not imply a different way of reading the text in this medium. There are many electronic texts which are simply printed texts put onto a screen, and these do not challenge readers any more than printed texts. More and more, however, electronic texts are being created which do more than duplicate print, and it is on the characteristics of these, more adventurous, texts that I will focus here.

Readers and texts can interact

Reading is often described as an interaction between a reader and a text. However, readers and printed texts cannot interact literally. A printed text cannot respond to a reader, nor do printed texts invite modification by a reader. To describe reading as an interaction simply reflects the fact that the outcomes of reading are the result of factors associated with the text and factors associated with the reader.

Because reading is interactive in this sense, a successful reader must be mentally active during reading. Readers clearly vary in their cognitive capabilities, and because of this a basic part of understanding the process of reading has come to be seen as understanding the reader. Features of printed texts, such as the use of illustrations, have not been ignored entirely, but it is true to say that the role of the printed text in the reading process has not generally been emphasised in discussion about the reading process. One reason for this greater interest in readers than in texts is that texts are static and inert once they are printed. When a writer's intended meaning is viewed as frozen in printed form, it is only logical to focus on a reader's efforts to construct meaning from this print.

Successful readers of printed texts know that it is their responsibility to derive meaning from those texts, and they approach the task of reading accordingly. A printed text cannot clarify itself if the reader is having difficulty understanding it. Readers may consciously interact with a text by applying their own knowledge to it, but they cannot carry on a dialogue with it.

Electronic texts, on the other hand, can involve a literal interaction between text and reader (Daniel and Reinking 1987). Using the capabilities of the computer, reading electronic texts can become a dialogue. Electronic texts can be programmed to adapt to an individual reader's needs and interests during reading which may, in turn, affect the strategies readers use to read and comprehend texts. One study (Reinking and Rickman 1990), for example, involved the use of electronic texts which provided readers, on request, with definitions of difficult words as they were reading. The effects of reading such texts were compared to the reading of printed texts accompanied by conventional resources such as dictionaries and glossaries. It was found that nine- to 13-year-olds reading the interactive computer texts investigated more word meanings, remembered the meanings of more words and understood more of the experimental text.

Other research (e.g. Reinking and Schreiner 1985) has suggested that readers' comprehension of texts increases when they read electronic texts providing a variety of support options, such as definitions of difficult words, illustrations, sometimes animated, of processes described, or maps of a text's structure.

In the future it will be possible to design electronic texts so that they respond to certain characteristics of the reader. Imagine a screen-based text that changes its format, content and speed of presentation depending on the rate at which a reader reads it. Possible already are texts which, at the end of each screen, ask the reader to choose what next to read. Interactive texts like these offer many potential texts. It would be possible to read them several times without reading exactly the same text twice.

Reading can be guided

The previous examples illustrate how electronic texts can respond to individual readers. This capability makes reading an interactive experience in which texts play an active role during reading. Not only can a computer present texts that respond to a reader, it can also determine which portion of a text a reader is permitted to see. Thus, electronic texts introduce the capability of influencing what a reader attends to *during* reading.

One example of how this feature might be used is the information text presented to readers one screen at a time. At the end of their reading of one screen, the readers are forced to respond to a question designed to judge their understanding of what they have read so far. Depending on their answers to these questions, the computer selects the next screen of text for them to read, thus allowing the possibility of reviewing misunderstood material or building upon existing understandings. Electronic text, therefore, can become a deliberate teaching tool.

Electronic texts have different structures

The idea that textual information might be structured differently if it is stored electronically is not new. In 1945, Vannevar Bush, a US presidential adviser, proposed that researchers develop electronic means for linking related information in a large database of microfilm documents. In 1960, Ted Nelson introduced the term *'hypertext'* in referring to electronic documents structured as non-linear, non-sequential texts (see Lunin and Rada 1989). Hypertexts have three attributes that separate them from conventionally structured printed texts:

- a database consisting of distinct units of text (which may consist of words, pictures, sounds or moving images);
- a network connecting the textual units (the textual units are referred to as 'nodes' in the network); and
- electronic tools for moving flexibly through the network.

The technology available when the concept of hypertext was first proposed did not allow easy and widespread implementation of the idea, but rapid developments in computing power over the past few years have made hypertexts not only possible but, through the medium of the internet and World Wide Web, virtually inescapable also. Web pages are coded in **HyperText** Markup Language – HTML.

Figure 9.1 shows an example of a simple web page on which some features of hypertext have been implemented (the live version of this page can be found at the following internet address – http://www.warwick.ac.uk/staff/D.J.Wray). This page contains a mixture of textual and graphic elements and is designed as the central node of a network of connecting texts. It contains seven points (hot spots) at which a mouse click will have the effect of moving the reader to a different node (web page) in the network (and one – the button marked 'Home' – which constantly brings the reader back to this node). These points are known as links and they can fulfil a range of functions in the overall hypertext. Those down the left-hand column in this example take the reader to completely separate pages, on each of which there are

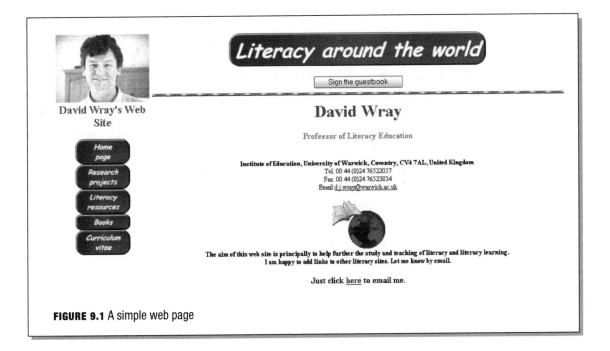

FIGURE 9.1 A simple web page

further choices to be made. To the right of the page, there are two links which both open up new windows on the screen to enable the reader to send an email. The third link, labelled 'Sign the guestbook', is, in essence, also an invitation to email the page's author but also gives something of a structure to this response.

An example of a much more complex web page can be found on the BBC website (http://www.bbc.co.uk). Here virtually every element on the page will, if clicked with the mouse, lead to a different page and some of these will produce sound and/or moving images.

The fact that electronic texts can be structured so differently from printed texts brings the difficulties inherent in electronic literacy into sharp focus. Becoming literate for electronic reading will require that readers become familiar with the non-linear, non-sequential text structures that are the natural form of electronic texts. They will also need to develop appropriate strategies for reading such texts. Reading web pages like the BBC home page is not straightforward and many otherwise skilful readers readily admit to getting lost quite easily within such material.

Electronic texts employ new symbols

Part of being literate is being good at using all the symbols that are available for communicating meaning in a written language. Readers and writers must know the conventions for using these symbols and understand how they convey meaning in a written language. Such awareness includes being able to use and interpret symbols beyond words themselves, such as graphic aids (e.g. illustrations and tables), organisational units (e.g. chapters) and typographical markers (e.g. underlining or italics).

Electronic texts can incorporate more symbols than printed texts. For example, symbols used with electronic texts, but not with printed texts, include: flashing, animated or moving visual displays; sound effects; and video. These elements create new possibilities for communicating meaning and they create the need for new conventions for using them in conjunction with traditional print.

The availability of more symbols is problematic in the development of electronic literacy, partly because agreed conventions for using the various symbols have not yet been established. Part of the problem is that the symbols available for use in electronic texts continue to expand rapidly, and the conventions for using them change with each advance in computer technology. To take a few examples, most literate people today will be familiar with the meanings of many of the symbols included in the screenshot in Figure 9.2. There may be some problematic symbols even here, in perhaps the most widely used computer writing environment in the world. This is especially true because the interface permits customisation so what we have here is the Word template which I, myself, use. Not every Word user will have defined the gluepot symbol (ninth symbol from the left on the top row of icons) to mean 'Select the whole document' – but it works for me.

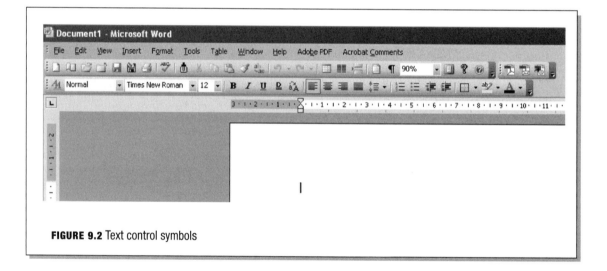

FIGURE 9.2 Text control symbols

Other sets of symbols may be more difficult. Figure 9.3, for example, shows a combination which will be very familiar to anyone who uses the Web as a source of information, yet its use is not easy. We know this is a PDF file (but probably not what those initials stand for), and we know that we need at least Acrobat Reader on our computers to read these files, but many people are not at all clear about how to navigate around such documents. Just what is the function of that little hand on the left of the toolbar? And why does that button with the binocular picture not immediately bring our view of the document closer? In fact, there are a number of ways to zoom in and out of the document using the selection of icons to the right of the tiny magnifying glass with the plus sign. These difficulties are magnified when you try to open the document on a different computer, because the software may have been set up differently and a quite different set of symbols may have been used.

FIGURE 9.3 Document control symbols

Less commonly used arrays of symbols may cause even more difficulties for a reader of electronic texts. Anyone who has a DVD-ROM drive in their computer (the vast majority nowadays) will probably have encountered the software whose interface appears in Figure 9.4.

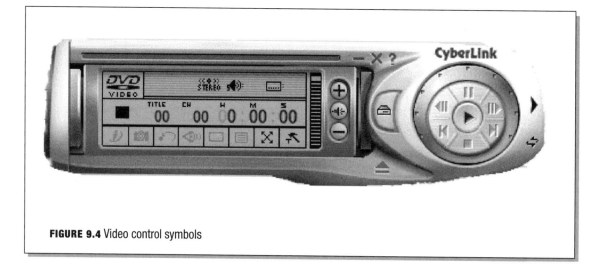

FIGURE 9.4 Video control symbols

This software allows us to play movie files, not just from inserted DVDs but also from our computer's internal storage, so some electronic texts may use it to integrate moving image material with other forms of text. Yet its particular symbols, I have to admit, I find cryptic. In a context where I am required to use this software, I am not as electronically literate as I could be.

An example of how electronic texts may change the relations between symbols is that in electronic texts graphic material is more closely integrated with prose. In printed materials, prose and graphic elements, such as tables, charts and diagrams, are more likely to be seen as separate symbol systems, each with its own symbols and conventions for using them. In electronic texts, however, prose, sounds and graphics may merge together. Think of a web page which, when opened, has text appearing at its foot and gradually scrolling up and eventually into the distance, rather like the opening sequence of the film *Star Wars*; only this is not in 'a galaxy far, far away': this is here, today, and is typical of the extra demands that reading electronic texts can make upon the reader.

Developing electronic literacy

The increasing use of electronic texts makes it clear that teachers need to begin to think seriously about how activities aimed at developing electronic literacy can be built into normal classroom literacy teaching. Ideally, these activities should meet three criteria:

1. They should help develop pupils' print-based literacy as well as their electronic literacy. Although electronic literacy is likely to become more and more important, it is unlikely, in the foreseeable future, that it will cause the demise of traditional literacy. Fortunately, the evidence is quite strongly supportive of the positive effects that experiences with electronic literacy can have upon pupils' print literacy.

2. They should involve authentic communication tasks for pupils. Enough is known about

the motivational and learning benefits for pupils seeing for themselves the purposes of reading and writing for us to be fairly confident that authenticity is a powerful benchmark of effectiveness in literacy work. Activities that feature electronic reading and writing have a head start in authenticity since most pupils will perceive these media as important in the world outside school.

3. They should engage pupils in critical thinking about the nature of printed and electronic texts as well as about the topics of these. As we have just seen there are some fundamental differences between these media, and pupils need to develop critical awareness of these, including when one is more appropriate than another, the effects of each upon the reader and the process of authorship appropriate to each.

In the following chapter I will explore some approaches to developing electronic literacy focused upon the writer. In the remainder of this chapter, I will discuss some uses of electronic literacy focused upon developing reading in pupils.

Electronic books

Some of the earliest reading materials available on the computer were adaptations of existing print texts. The American companies Discis (*Thomas' Snowsuit, The Paperbag Princess*) and Broderbund (*Arthur's Teacher Troubles, Just Grandma and Me*) were the first to have any major impact. These were simply collections of books which had been converted to work from CD-ROM. Of course, they were not just placed on a CD; they were enhanced to harness the power of the computer. Each CD contained a multimedia book which would read itself to a child while sound effects and music complemented the story. The books presented many options, such as varying speeds of reading, explanations of words and even options to have the book read in a different language. The idea was that, as a child's reading ability grew, he/she could use the computer just to say the words he/she could not read.

Later, British companies such as Sherston Software began to produce much smaller 'Talking Books', each title being compressed to fit on a single floppy disk. The simplicity of the Sherston system meant that these books had a major impact in UK schools, especially when the best-selling British reading scheme, *Oxford Reading Tree*, adopted the system to produce electronic versions of its books.

Most electronic books produced for school use have similar facilities. They all provide on-screen text, illustrated with pictures. By clicking on certain icons the text can be read aloud by the computer, or the pictures can be animated. They all also provide the facility for the reader to click on individual words (phrases in the case of the American books) to hear these read aloud.

A number of research studies have investigated the impact of such electronic stories on children's reading. Medwell, for example, (1996, 1998) explored whether talking books could help young children learn to read traditional, print texts, and if so, how they supported children's reading. In Medwell's studies, Reception/Year 1 pupils were studied as they used the Sherston *Naughty Stories* and the Oxford Reading Tree *Talking Stories*. The results of these two studies suggested that talking books do help young children to learn to read traditional texts and that they particularly helped children to understand the meanings of the stories. Medwell found that children who used the electronic versions of the books learned more than children who only used print versions, but that the most effective learning was achieved by children who read the print versions with their teachers and then used the electronic versions by themselves. This suggests that, although electronic books can help pupils progress in reading, they complement rather than replace the role of the skilled teacher of reading.

Research, therefore, seems to suggest that electronic books can help pupils develop as readers, but that they need to be used circumspectly by teachers if the maximum impact is to be obtained.

Finding out with the computer

In many ways, information text was made for computerised presentation. Most readers do not read information books in the linear way they may approach fiction text, and adopt instead a pseudo-hypertextual approach, focused around the core node of the contents or index page, from which links are made to other text units. Having such text on a computer simply makes such an approach more efficient. Rather than having to physically turn the pages of a book, the reader can just click on a link to move to the relevant information.

One of the unfortunate by-products of this is that the already significant tendency of pupils to copy from information books is likely to be worsened by the use of electronic information text. After all, selecting, copying and pasting material from a CD-ROM or from the internet is a lot easier than having, physically, to write out material from a book. There are a number of tried-and-tested strategies for helping pupils avoid straight copying when they use information books, and these work just as well with computer-based material.

A systematic treatment of ways to avoid pupils copying information text can be found in Wray and Lewis (1997). They recommend thinking about information finding as a series of mental processes, an analysis they refer to as the EXIT (EXtending Interactions with Texts) model (see Figure 9.5).

Crucial to avoiding copying is the thinking that pupils are encouraged to do *before* they begin to use information sources. Wray and Lewis recommend getting pupils to consider what they already know about a topic before formulating some questions to which they would like to find answers. This then lessens the possibility of them approaching information sources looking to record everything they find. A particularly useful strategy here is to ask pupils to use grids such as the KWL (see Figure 4.3) to record the process of their information research.

Wray and Lewis also suggest that, when pupils are reading information text, they read actively. One strategy for active reading is for readers to mark text which they think is significant. In printed text this can involve the use of highlighter pens and there is usually an equivalent to this for screen-based text. In Microsoft Word this involves clicking the Text Highlight button, selecting a highlight colour and then using the mouse to select appropriate

Process stages	Questions
1. Activation of previous knowledge	1. What do I already know about this subject?
2. Establishing purposes	2. What do I need to find out and what will I do with the information?
3. Locating information	3. Where and how will I get this information?
4. Adopting an appropriate strategy	4. How should I use this source of information to get what I need?
5. Interacting with text	5. What can I do to help me understand this better?
6. Monitoring understanding	6. What can I do if there are parts I don't understand?
7. Making a record	7. What should I make a note of from this information?
8. Evaluating information	8. Which items of information should I believe and which should I keep an open mind about?
9. Assisting memory	9. How can I help myself remember the important parts?
10. Communicating information	10. How should I let other people know about this?

FIGURE 9.5 The EXIT model: stages and questions

text. More than one colour can be used in the same document, thus allowing information relevant to a number of questions to be picked out.

Another active reading strategy is for pupils to restructure the information they read into one of a variety of other forms. Pupils might go to information sources armed with a pre-drawn grid which will both guide them in their information search and help them structure the information they find for subsequent reporting. An example of this with print text research is the grid in Figure 4.10 which was used by some Year 3 pupils to help them find information about home life in Ancient Greece.

With electronic text, pupils might be given a word-processed grid to keep open in a window on the screen while they browse information sources in another window. Noting information on the grid can then be done using the keyboard, and the results can be printed out and shared.

Problem-solving with texts

There are a range of textual problem-solving activities (generically referred to as DARTs – Directed Activities Relating to Texts) which have been shown to be useful ways of encouraging pupils to interact purposefully with printed texts. Activities in this range include cloze, where pupils have to work together to suggest possible words to fill deletions in a text, and sequencing, where a group of pupils have to work out a meaningful order for a text which has been cut into sections and mixed up. All these activities involve group discussion of disrupted texts and their main aim is to recreate meaningful text.

An early attempt to adapt activities like this to electronic text was the computer program known as Developing TRAY. This program was written initially for use with secondary, slow-reading pupils. The name derives from the idea of a print gradually coming into focus in a photographer's developing tray. Starting with a screen showing only punctuation and a series of dashes to represent letters, the pupils gradually reconstruct the extract, initially by 'buying' letters, then by predicting words or phrases as the text becomes clearer. A number of research studies, both at secondary (e.g. Johnston 1985) and primary (Haywood and Wray 1988) levels, have suggested that experience with the program involves the use of high-level problem-solving skills, analysis of data, decision-making about strategies, the creation and interpretation of meaning, and hypothesis-forming and testing.

TRAY is now 20 years old, which for educational software is indeed old, but the fact that a modernised version is still available is testimony to its abiding usefulness in developing pupils' reading. It is usually found now as part of text problem-solving suites of programs (often given names such as 'word detectives') which include computer versions of other DARTs.

A more recent addition to teachers' technological armouries is the interactive whiteboard, which has a great deal of potential in the teaching of reading. The whiteboard allows the information appearing on a computer screen to be projected onto a much larger surface, but when it is there it can be interacted with, i.e. text can be added with a pen, moved, annotated or deleted. This means that the interactivity which is characteristic of electronic text can now be carried out as a shared activity with large groups of pupils. A simple example of this is the sequencing activity mentioned briefly earlier. Normally this is done with sections of printed text that have been cut up, and pupils move the sections around, experimenting with possible orders until they find one they can agree on. Because of the size of the text and the need to handle the sections, it is normal for this activity to involve three or four pupils at most. With an interactive whiteboard, however, the sections of text appear in large type on the board and each can be moved around using the board pen. This makes whole-class discussion of a text in this way possible.

Literacy software is beginning to appear to exploit the potential of the interactive whiteboard. One package, *Easiteach Literacy* (Wray and Medwell 2003), supplies teachers with a large range of texts for shared work, and the software includes tools such as highlighter pens, instant cloze text-makers and a range of word and phonic banks.

Conclusion

In this chapter I have explored some of the ways in which text is changing with the advent of new technologies. Central to my argument here is that as text is changing so the process of reading changes also. Reading electronic texts is not the same as reading printed texts, which means that teaching pupils to read needs to develop too. In the final section of the chapter, I briefly examined some teaching approaches involving electronic texts. Inevitably, however, teaching lags behind the world outside and it is certain that we have only just begun to respond in schools to the changing nature of text. There are exciting changes still to come.

Writing electronic texts

Introduction

For a number of reasons, writing was one of the first aspects to be significantly affected by the development of personal computers and other new technologies. The vast majority of the writing that gets done in the world – at least the commercial world – today is done through the medium of information technology. The sheer prominence of screen-, as opposed to paper-, based writing means that we need to familiarise children with the skills and possibilities of this new medium if they are to use it confidently in their lives. But ICT also makes possible a number of beneficial approaches to the *teaching* of writing. Evidence suggests that the use of computers as tools for writing can significantly enhance children's understanding of, and competence in, all forms of writing. The National Curriculum requires teachers to make sure that 'pupils should have opportunities to plan and review their writing, assembling and developing their ideas on paper and on screen'.

ICT has, therefore, a dual role in teaching and developing writing. On the one hand, it can effectively help children learn how to write in *traditional* forms; on the other, it extends these forms by adding new possibilities for writing. In this chapter I will explore some of the possibilities of both these roles. I will begin by looking closely at the predominant writing tool offered by ICT, the word-processor.

Using word-processors

How can a word-processor help?

Many teachers have been impressed by the way even quite young children learn quickly how to use word-processing programs on the computer, and seem to be able to improve the quality of their writing by doing so. What is it about word-processors that leads to this improvement?

To answer this question we need, first, to look at the ways in which our understanding of the process of writing has changed over the last few years. Perhaps the most significant feature of this change has been the realisation that to expect children to produce well-thought-out, interesting writing, correctly spelled and punctuated, grammatical and neatly written, at one sitting, is to expect the impossible. Even experienced adult writers do not work that way, and will confirm that any writing other than the most trivial goes through several drafts before it is considered finished. Many teachers encourage their pupils to approach writing in this way, that is to write drafts which can then be revised, shared with other readers, discussed and edited, before reaching their final versions. At Key Stage 2, the National Curriculum requires that pupils be given opportunities to do this, and spells out the process in some detail:

Pupils should be taught to:

- **plan** – note and develop initial ideas;
- **draft** – develop ideas from the plan into structured written text;
- **revise** – alter and improve the draft;
- **proofread** – check the draft for spelling and punctuation errors, omissions or repetitions;
- **present** – prepare a neat, correct and clear final copy.

The use of the word-processor as a writing tool reinforces this drafting process. Writing on a computer screen does not have the permanence of writing on paper. Everything about it becomes provisional, and can be altered at the touch of a key. This provisional nature of word-processed writing has very important implications for the way children think about and set about their writing.

A significant reason why children may find it difficult to really accept the idea of writing as provisional when it is done on paper is the fact that, if they wish to change their writing, this will usually involve rewriting it. The sheer physical effort of this will persuade some children to adopt a much more studied, once-and-for-all approach to their writing. With a word-processor, however, alterations can be made on the screen and there is no need to rewrite. This facility for immediate error correction allows children to approach writing much more exper-imentally. They soon become prepared to try things out and alter them several times if need be. They also begin to be able to live with uncertainty. If, for example, they are unsure of particular spellings, they can try an approximation and check it later, without breaking the flow of their writing ideas. 'We'll do the spellings afterwards' becomes a familiar strategy.

An example of this provisionality in writing can be seen in the following two versions of a story written by a six-year-old girl.

Version 1
once upon a time there was a baby called henry and a big dragon too and a boy called tom and a girl called sarah and the baby and the big dragon took them to the world of darkness and tom was scared but sarah said its spooky and scary but the nice dragons said wheel keep you safe and that is there best one

Version 2
Once upon a time there was a baby dragon called henry and a big dragon called peter. They had so many adventures but there best one is when they made friends with a boy called tom and a girl called sarah. The baby and the big dragon took them to the frightening world of darkness and tom was scared. Sarah said its spooky and scary but the friendly dragons said wheel keep you safe and they did. That is there best adventure.

The first version she wrote by herself on paper, and then typed into a word-processor. It is a fairly typical infant story with an unadventurous use of words, no punctuation and a plot which seems not to have been thought through. The second version, which she produced after about 20 minutes on the computer, suggests, however, that some of these judgements about her writing ability may have been harsh. Here, her range of vocabulary increases, the technical aspects of her writing improve, and her plot, while still not outstanding, at least shows an attempt to take into consideration the needs of a reader. The computer allowed her space to experiment and also to step back from her writing and read it with fresh eyes. These two features are perhaps the most significant of the benefits that word-processing gives to children's writing.

Another significant feature provided by word-processing is the facility to cut and paste text electronically. Sections of text can easily be moved around the piece of writing. This allows writers to re-sequence their writing with little effort and to experiment with different sequences.

An example of this can be seen in the following story written by two six-year-olds after reading *A Troll at School* by Elizabeth Walker.

> Once upon a time a troll lived in a bucket of paint. One day he went to my friends school and he bit my friends hand and she shouted miss brown that is her teacher. Her teacher said go to the head teacher. My friend is called Sarah. The head teacher said sit on the prickly mat. Then it was time to go home and when we went to bed we heard noises going like this bump bump bump bump bump and bump. Guess who it was. You are right it was the troll. He was green and slimy with red eyes.

After discussing this with their teacher, they agreed that it would improve their story if two sentences were moved to different places. This was done with eight key presses on the word-processor.

> Once upon a time a troll lived in a bucket of paint. He was green and slimy with red eyes. One day he went to my friend Sarah's school and he bit my friends hand and she shouted miss brown that is her teacher. Her teacher said go to the head teacher. The head teacher said sit on the prickly mat. Then it was time to go home and when we went to bed we heard noises going like this bump bump bump bump bump and bump. Guess who it was. You are right it was the troll.

It is, of course, possible to achieve this with pencil and paper by using arrows, or with scissors and glue, but neither of these methods compares with the simplicity of the word-processor. Again, this facility increases the provisionality of writing. Not only can text be changed at will, but it can also be rearranged in any number of ways. The full benefits of this will be seen later in the chapter when we discuss desktop publishing.

Most word-processors also have the facility to search through texts for particular words or markers, and then replace them with other words. This can assist children's writing in a variety of ways. First, it allows them to change their minds easily. If, for example, they have written a story about a boy called Pete and suddenly decide they really want it to be about a girl called Mary, these details can be altered throughout the text by a couple of key presses.

Secondly, it provides a way of dealing easily with consistent misspellings. If, for example, a child regularly spells 'occasion' as 'ocassion', or 'should' as 'sholud', he can be asked to check these words after finishing his writing. Having ascertained the correct spelling, he can then use the word-processor to alter every occurrence of the misspelling at one go. Most word-processors allow the user to decide whether each individual occurrence should be altered. Usually the user has to press 'Y' or 'N' as appropriate. This can be useful if there are words the child confuses regularly, such as 'there' and 'their', or 'hear' and 'here'. Being asked to consider each one in turn encourages children to become more aware of the contexts in which each one is appropriate.

A further use of the search-and-replace facility is to eliminate some of the distraction caused when children search for the spellings of words they are unsure of. These can be entered at first using a marker. When the first draft is done, the children can then find the correct spellings and use the replace facility to change their markers.

An example of this use of spelling markers can be seen in the following short piece. The child first wrote:

> Once upon a time there was a slimy t** who lived in a paint pot. This t** was f** but he was only f** with people who were f** with him. With other people the t** was fierce.

The spellings of 'troll' and 'friendly' were then checked, and the replace facility used to produce:

> Once upon a time there was a slimy troll who lived in a paint pot. This troll was friendly but he was only friendly with people who were friendly with him. With other people the troll was fierce.

This is an extremely useful technique in writing, and once children understand it they can use it to save themselves a great deal of writing effort. Frequently used words can also be entered as markers, and typed once in full at the end of the writing. This was how the writer wrote the word 'word-processor' in the present chapter.

A further important feature of word-processing has already been hinted at. If a piece of writing can be saved to disk, it can then be re-read and re-edited at a later date. The facility to edit previously created text has a very important effect. Writing ceases to be a one-shot exercise, with everything having to be done correctly at one sitting. There is, in fact, no limit to the number of times the writer can return to it and make changes as easily as the first time. This adds to writing the important dimension of time. Ideas can be considered over time, new ideas can be taken on board and writing can be discussed with others. This has the effect of making writing a much more thoughtful process.

Allowing children the time for the reflective editing implied by this may seem to involve the dedication of large amounts of computer time to very few children. This, however, need not be so because of the facility to print out the writing that the children produce. They can then take away this print-out, and work on revising it away from the computer. This can involve crossing sections out, scribbling extra ideas in and discussing the draft with anyone they wish. They can then return to the computer when it is again free, to call up their draft and make any changes to it they feel necessary, before printing again. This process can then be repeated.

Using hard copy for initial revision has an extra advantage in addition to freeing computer time for others to use. By altering printed text, and especially by crossing out, children can begin to lose their fear of making writing messy. Because of their earlier educational experience, many children approach writing under what has been termed 'the tyranny of the flawless page'. They are extremely reluctant to do anything to disturb this flawlessness. A print-out, however, has cost them little physical effort and can always be repeated if need be. It need not, therefore, be kept flawless. This change in children's attitudes towards writing has great significance for their future approach to it, and helps convince them of the provisional nature of writing.

There is, of course, little point in using a word-processor with children unless their work can be printed out. Print-outs are available, however, not in single but in multiple copies, which can be of immense benefit. It is a simple matter to take sufficient copies of a piece of writing for the child to have one to go in a folder, the teacher to have one to display, one to be placed in the child's record portfolio and one to be taken home to parents. The significance of this is readily seen by considering what happens with non-word-processed writing which a teacher wishes to put on display. Often this results in the child having to copy it out, with consequent negative effects on that child's motivation to write.

A further advantage of printed writing is its levelling effect. Many children have poor self-images of themselves as writers, not because they lack ability in the composing aspects of the process, but because they simply find handwriting a strain. In word-processing, poor hand-writing is no longer a problem. Children with poor physical co-ordination can write as well as those with good, and the sense of achievement these children get can be enormous. This is not to argue, of course, that clear, efficient handwriting is no longer necessary. Children will still need to be taught handwriting. It does mean, though, that lack of ability in this aspect of writing need not assume the overarching, debilitating effects it often does. It also means that teachers can get beyond the presentation aspects of children's writing when attempting to make judgements about children's abilities. Most children will need help of some kind with their writing, but it is easy for teachers to concentrate this help on the physical aspect simply because this is what stands out immediately. If this aspect can be discounted, teachers can direct their help to other, more important, parts of the writing process.

Children's word-processed text can be rearranged in various ways on the computer. This makes it possible for their writing to emerge looking very much like that in 'real' books, with consequent benefits for their motivation to write. The aspect of this which is usually discovered first is justification, the effects of which can be seen in the following example of the writing of a six-year-old. Her story first looked like this:

> once there was a dragon called Ace he was a friendly dragon and Ace met a boy called john and the dragon said will you have a fight with me because if you do and you win I will take you for a ride yes said John I will have a fight against you John won the fight and the dragon took John for a ride to the moon they came back with straw so they did not hurt themselves.

This was then corrected and (justified) to produce this:

> Once there was a dragon called Ace. He was a friendly dragon. Ace met a boy called John and the dragon said, will you have a fight with me? Because if you do and you win I will take you for a ride.

Yes, said John. I will have a fight against you. John won the fight and the dragon took John for a ride to the moon. They came back with straw so they did not hurt themselves.

The child was delighted with the look of this and commented that it was just like in her reading book.

This ability to rearrange text can be taken further by altering the format of the text. If the writing had been done for a class newspaper, it could be formatted with narrower columns.

Once there was a dragon called Ace. He was a friendly dragon. Ace met a boy called John and the dragon said, will you have a fight with me? Because if you do and you win I will take you for a ride. Yes, said John. I will have a fight against you. John won the fight and the dragon took John for a ride to the moon. They came back with straw so they did not hurt themselves.

Most word-processors also permit writing to be produced in a variety of type styles, or fonts, from Script to Gothic. So the above story might be produced as:

Once there was a dragon called Ace. He was a friendly dragon. Ace met a boy called John and the dragon said, will you have a fight with me? Because if you do and you win I will take you for a ride. Yes, said John. I will have a fight against you. John won the fight and the dragon took John for a ride to the moon. They came back with straw so they did not hurt themselves.

or:

Once there was a dragon called Ace. He was a friendly dragon. Ace met a boy called John and the dragon said, will you have a fight with me? Because if you do and you win I will take you for a ride. Yes, said John. I will have a fight against you. John won the fight and the dragon took John for a ride to the moon. They came back with straw so they did not hurt themselves.

Such features can enhance children's writing a great deal, and all have the effect of making children enjoy writing more.

Word-processors can be used as writing tools for individual children. This is, however, an uneconomic use of expensive equipment and does not make best use of their particular features. Because writing appears on what looks like a television screen it is much more public than the usual pencil-and-paper process. It positively invites sharing. A more usual way of using the word-processor is for children to write in collaboration with one or two of their classmates. This enables discussion and debate to take place about the writing, which has an almost inevitable beneficial effect upon the quality of what is produced.

In fact, improved quality in writing is the chief reason for the use of word-processors with children. There are several reasons why this happens, one of which, the opportunity for discussion and debate, has already been referred to. There is also the distancing effect word-processors seem to have; they allow children to stand back from their writing and read it with fresh eyes. This distancing permits them to make changes they would, perhaps, otherwise not realise were necessary.

Word-processors can also be used as teaching devices in the context of children's writing, with consequent improvements in quality. An example of this can be seen in the following piece written jointly by two seven-year-olds. After hunting for minibeasts in the school field, the two boys wrote:

today we went out side to look for little creatures and we found an ant and one was red and jamie russ found a big black spider and daniel jones caught it in his pot and we also caught a centipede and it was red and it went very fast and mrs wilkins caught a earwig and two caterpillars but one caretpillar escaped from the yoggat pot and we found some slugs and they made a slimy trail on the white paper

Their teacher asked them to read the piece to her, and they were all struck by the over-use of the word 'and'. The teacher used the search-and-replace facility of the word-processor to exchange the 'ands' for markers and asked them to look at the writing again.

today we went out side to look for little creatures *** we found a ant *** one was red *** jamie russ found a big black spider *** daniel jones caught it in his pot *** we also caught a centipede *** it was red *** it went very fast *** mrs wilkins caught a earwig *** two caterpillars but one caretpillar escaped from the yoggat pot *** we found some slugs *** they made a slimy trail on the white paper

This revision produced the following finished article:

Today we went out side to look for little creatures and we found ants. One of them was red. Just then Jamie Russ found a big black spider. Then daniel jones caught it in his pot. We also caught a centipede. The centipede was red like the ant. The centipede went very fast like the ant. Mrs Wilkins caught an earwig and two caterpillars but one escaped from the pot. Then we found some slugs and they made a slimy trail on the white paper.

The improvement in quality is quite clear. This may have happened without the use of the word-processor but it is doubtful that the process would have been so simple, or the children so eager to do it.

There are, therefore, several excellent reasons why word-processors should feature prominently in the writing experience of primary children. Of course, as with any teaching materials, it is the manner of use of this new tool which is the crucial factor. In the next section, therefore, we will discuss strategies for using word-processors in the classroom.

Ways of using word-processors

The word-processor as a typewriter

A fairly common way of using a word-processor in the classroom, especially when the teacher and children are new to it, is to dedicate it to the task of producing fair copies of children's writing. In this mode of use, children write their pieces in the traditional way, and when these are judged suitable, they are allowed to type them into the computer. Sometimes, for speed, the teacher will assist with this typing.

There are, of course, several advantages in this mode of use. Word-processed writing is neat and professional-looking, typing it in is a reasonably quick task, and the teacher can help things along by taking a turn at the typing, even when the children are not there. Moreover, because not every piece of writing can be typed in, the use of the word-processor can be seen as a reward for children who produce good writing, and this, therefore, gives children an incentive to try harder with their writing.

There are, however, some problems as well. The writing that is typed into the word-processor is already 'final draft'; that is, it has been considered, maybe revised and edited before it reaches the computer. The ease of doing exactly these things, however, is the major benefit to be gained from using the word-processor. Therefore the computer is not being used to its best advantage.

Neither is the elitism of this mode of use helpful. If using the word-processor is a reward for doing good writing, children who have problems with writing (who can be the majority in a class) will get insufficient use of the computer for it to be of help to them. And, as was pointed out in the previous section, help them it can, if only by allowing them space to experiment with their writing and instantly abandon experiments which do not work. Using the word-processor as a typewriter does not encourage this experimentation, and, in this way, misses the real point of the activity.

The word-processor as a composing tool

Of far more benefit is the use of the word-processor as a tool for composition rather than simply transcription. This implies children using the computer for the whole of the writing process – from the initial jotting down of ideas to writing a first draft to revising and editing this draft to finally printing a finished piece.

Of course, using the word-processor in this way is very intensive of computer time. The groups need a great deal of time in front of the screen. This can be cut down if the pupils are encouraged to make regular printouts of their work and take them away to discuss and revise, but there will be occasions when children need to reflect while looking at their writing on the computer screen, to try things out and consider the results, and to talk about what they are doing as they are doing it. Because of these demands upon time, and of the other children in the class who also need their turn, it makes most sense to involve children in writing in groups rather than as individuals. This has positive benefits in that it ensures children will discuss their writing, with consequent improvements in quality.

Shared writing with a word-processor

A word-processor can be used as a medium for shared writing, although, of course, the presentation device used will need to be sufficiently large for the writing on it to be read easily by the whole class. This requires either a very large computer screen (a 21-inch screen may just be large enough), a data projector to project the computer image onto a large screen or wall, or an electronic whiteboard.

Here are a few examples of possible shared writing lessons that teachers might adapt for their own purposes:

1. Word-level work – Year 4

Objective: to spell regular verb endings *s, ed, ing*.

Set the word-processor to display a large font, e.g. 28-point, and type in the following list of words: *care, come, face, file, give, glue, hope, ice, joke, like, live, love, make.* Type *ing* after the first few, using a different font. Explain the rule about dropping the final *e*, and delete the spaces between the word and the suffix. Finally, delete the *e* as well, giving a dynamic demonstration of how the joining of stem and suffix and the deletion of the final *e* are part of the same action. Do this with a couple of examples.

give *ing*	**give** *ing*	*give*ing	*giving*
hope *ing*	**hope** *ing*	hope*ing*	hop*ing*

Now let individual children come to the computer to carry out the same action. If you have a talking word-processor you can listen to the sounds of the words and then compare them to some common spelling mistakes such as 'comming' and 'hopping'.

2. Sentence-level work – Year 4

Objective: to identify common adverbs with a *-ly* suffix.

Set the word-processor to display a large font, e.g. 28-point, and type in the following list of *-ly* adverbs: *quickly, slowly, swiftly, sluggishly, rapidly, unhurriedly*. Highlight the 'ly' and then increasing the size (on most word-processors this can be done by holding down Ctrl + Shift and > (greater than), and decreasing the size is achieved by holding down Ctrl + Shift and < (less than)).

quickly   *quickly*   *quickly*   *quickly*

Let some pupils try this with other words. Such animations are a good way of fixing certain letter strings in pupils' minds.

3. Sentence-level work – Year 3

Objective: to recognise the function of verbs in sentences, and to use verb tenses in writing.

Use a large font size and write some simple sentences without their verbs, e.g.

'Alexander all the chocolate bars.'

Ask the pupils what is missing. Where should the missing word go? What possibilities are there for this missing word or phrase? Type one suggestion into the sentence, using a font which stands out. Use copy-and-paste to reproduce the same sentence five or so times. In each sentence, use a different verb, or a variation on the same verb.

*Alexander **ate** all the chocolate bars.*
*Alexander **grabbed** all the chocolate bars.*
*Alexander **hated** all the chocolate bars.*
*Alexander **will eat** all the chocolate bars.*
*Alexander **eats** all the chocolate bars.*
*Alexander **has eaten** all the chocolate bars.*

Discuss all the different meanings that this creates. Pupils should now be in a position to write their own versions of this changing sentence.

As an extension to this activity, you could try adding adverbs (Year 4 – identify adverbs and . . . notice where they occur in sentences and how they are used to qualify the meanings of verbs). Does a different position affect the meaning of the sentence?

*Alexander **quickly** ate all the chocolate bars.*
***Quickly**, Alexander ate all the chocolate bars.*
*Alexander ate all the chocolate bars **quickly**.*

4. Sentence-level work – Year 5

Objective: to investigate clauses through understanding how clauses are connected.

Have on the screen/whiteboard some examples of jumbled sentences, that is sentences in which the main and subordinate clauses do not match.

Walking slowly along the road, Libby finally forced herself out of bed.
When Mum shouted upstairs, James suddenly heard the hoot of a car behind him.

Discuss these sentences and demonstrate how, using 'drag and drop' or 'cut and paste', they can be sorted out.

Try moving the subordinate clause to a different position in the sentence, and discuss any changes to the meaning that this causes.

Walking slowly along the road, James suddenly heard the hoot of a car behind him.
James suddenly heard the hoot of a car behind him, walking slowly along the road.

Pupils can then be asked to construct their complex sentences using this pattern, and experiment with different clause positioning.

5. Text-level work – Year 6

Objective: to use different genres as models to write.

Have on the screen/whiteboard an extract from a pre-twentieth-century text. Read this with the class and discuss what makes it rather difficult to read. Show them how you are able to change difficult words and/or phrases for simpler, more modern equivalents. For example, the following extract from *Treasure Island*:

'Well, then,' said he, 'this is the berth for me. Here you matey,' he cried to the man who trundled the barrow; `bring up alongside and help up my chest. I'll stay here a bit,' he continued. 'I'm a plain man; rum and bacon and eggs is what I want, and that head up there for to watch ships off. What you mought call me? You mought call me captain. Oh, I see what you're at – there;' and he threw down three or four gold pieces on the threshold. 'You can tell me when I've worked through that,' says he, looking as fierce as a commander.

might become:

'Well, then,' he said, `this is the place for me. Here you mate,' he cried to the man who pushed the cart; 'come here and help up my chest. I'll stay here a bit,' he continued. 'I'm a plain man; rum and bacon and eggs are what I want, and that cliff up there to watch for ships. What should you call me? You should call me captain. Oh, I see what you want – there;' and he threw down three or four gold pieces on the counter. 'You can tell me when I've used all that up,' he said, looking as fierce as a commander.

They could continue this activity later in groups.

Guided writing with word-processors

A group involved in guided writing can work in pairs on a writing task with the guidance they need having already been set up on their computers. There are a number of ways of achieving this:

1. Use computer versions of writing frames (Lewis and Wray 1997) to scaffold writing in particular forms. Electronic versions of frames can very easily be altered and extended by teachers or pupils.

For the 'Story' genre, for instance, you might begin with a frame which provides a lot of support:

Once upon a time there were three . . .

There was a Mummy, a Daddy and a . . .

They all lived in a little house in the . . .

Later, the support can be reduced and variations in openings and link words can be encouraged.

From a distance the island seemed . . .

When we got closer, however, . . .

We landed on a sandy beach and . . .

Exploring the island, we discovered . . .

A development from writing frames is the use of starter paragraphs. For storywriting, these might take the form of two paragraphs from different parts of the story, the pupils' task being to insert the text which goes between them. For example:

She got out of bed very quietly, opened the door without a squeak and started to walk down the passage. She could hear her Grandma snoring. She moved very carefully and very slowly. Finally she found the door to the kitchen. It opened with a gentle creak.

The dog barked ferociously as she climbed back over the wall. She took no notice. She held the parcel carefully under one arm and dropped down into the garden.

2. Electronic frames might also include pop-up comments with extra vocabulary lists (in Microsoft Word, this can be achieved by 'Insert – Comment' on the toolbar). A similar effect can be achieved by including hypertext links which, when clicked, produce vocabulary lists (type 'Control + K' and then the name of the file of vocabulary).

3. Provide differentiated support through the use of hidden prompts that a child can access as he/she works. In Microsoft Word, text can be marked as 'hidden' and is only revealed when the 'Show/Hide' button is clicked (this button usually has the symbol ¶ on it). A writing frame such as the following might be used to guide the writing of a set of instructions (the italicised text would be hidden).

You are going to write instructions for learning to do archery.

Learning to do archery

List the equipment you needed here – you could use bullet points for each item:
Equipment needed:

Now think of any rules or instructions you were given. Imagine you are explaining these to someone who has never done this activity. What tense will you write in?
First,

Next,

Then,

Finally,

Now complete your instructions by writing some guidelines on how to pack away and care for the equipment you have used.

FIGURE 10.1 A computer-based writing frame

4. Ask pupils to manipulate text which has already been entered into the computer. For example, if the objective of the activity is for pupils to organise letters into simple paragraphs (Y3 T3 T23), the teaching point is paragraphing, not writing a letter, so time would be saved in presenting pupils with a range of letters they were required to paragraph.

5. Use specially designed commercial software to support writing (I Can Write, from Resource Education, and Clicker 4, from Crick Software, are two packages that are based upon the writing frame idea).

Group work with word-processors: some suggested activities

Pupils can:

- select and drag text to match rhyming words, to complete sentences, to unscramble muddled sentences etc.;

- identify different categories of words, e.g. highlighting all nouns pink, all pronouns green etc.;

- alter existing text using, for example, alternative adjectives, verbs, synonyms etc., and using different coloured text for any changes;

- use cut-and-paste to reinstate the correct order of a short story in which the order of the paragraphs has been changed;

- use the Find and Replace function (Control + K in Microsoft Word) to replace overused words such as 'said' and 'nice';

- use the Find function on its own to search for common spelling patterns, e.g. all words ending in 'ing' or containing 'ea';

Desktop publishing

In the world outside schools the last 15 years have seen the dramatic growth of the use of computer systems for desktop publishing, that is the production of books, journals, newspapers etc. by writers themselves, without the intermediate stage of specialist typesetting. The technology to make this possible had a vast impact in the commercial world, especially on those sections of the workforce such as print workers whose skills were thereby made redundant.

The potential of this technology has also been realised by schools, many of whom were quick to see the potential of desktop publishing as a vehicle for the production of their children's work. Desktop publishing can be seen as providing extra facilities for the output of children's work on the computer. Several of these facilities have important implications.

The first concerns purpose. Because of some of the features discussed below, an important use of desktop publishing is in the production of class/school newspapers or magazines. These by their nature are intended for other people to read, and their producers are therefore involved in 'public' writing. This adds a dimension of purposefulness to writing which children may occasionally not perceive in their other writing tasks. The public nature of this writing in turn gives children greater incentive to improve its quality and accuracy. Public writing implies also that an audience has to be taken into account. Children who are aware that what they produce is going to be read by a variety of other people can be alerted to the needs of these audiences, and encouraged to reconsider the form and content of their writing in the light of these needs.

A further feature of the production of newspapers and magazines through desktop publishing is that these media are generally very familiar to children. They recognise their distinctive features and appreciate the facility that desktop publishing gives them to emulate these 'real life' features. An important stage in the production of a class newspaper or magazine should be the close study by children of published ones. In the course of this study, many literacy skills can be taught and practised, from the critical reading of advertisements to the factors influencing the impact of headlines. Children may also be introduced to other features, although from experience in using desktop publishing packages with children, it appears they are already much more aware than might be imagined of the importance of such features as the typeface used, the design of the layout or the style of writing demanded in particular formats. Likewise, one of the benefits of using these packages with children is a sharpening of this awareness.

The desktop publishing environment has some features which make it particularly useful for realistic writing formats. One of the most important of these is the cut-and-paste facility. By using this, sections of pages can be electronically lifted from one place and moved or copied to another. This is an extension of the provisionality of writing mentioned earlier. Anything children produce can always be changed in a number of ways, and they quickly grasp the power of this, and experiment with format.

Another feature which desktop publishing makes possible is the mixing of text and pictures. Users can grab pictures from camcorders and digital cameras, and import these into the desktop publishing environment. Once under the control of the computer software, these pictures can be manipulated in various ways: stretched, enlarged, reduced, rotated, reversed, chopped into pieces and overlaid or interspersed with text. This is a facility of immense potential, which enables users of small personal computers to produce pages which are almost indistinguishable from those of real newspapers.

One group of Year 5 pupils used their class digital camera to take pictures of some toys. These pictures were then imported into Word to illustrate a story they wrote collaboratively for the Year 2 class in their school. One page from this story is given in Figure 10.2.

Hypertexts

New technology also makes possible a kind of writing which could not be done using traditional print and paper methods. We have all become very familiar, through our use of the internet, with the texts which characterise the World Wide Web – hypertexts. Traditional texts are usually designed to be read in one way. They are linear, with a well-defined start and a

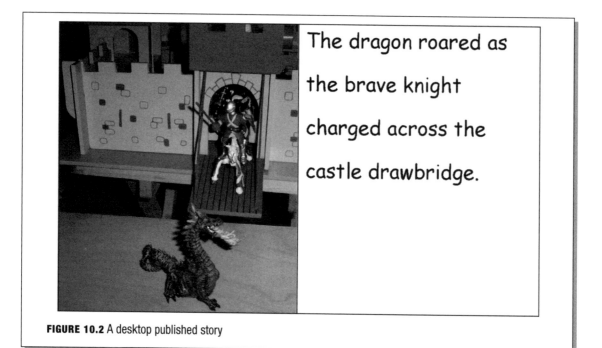

The dragon roared as the brave knight charged across the castle drawbridge.

FIGURE 10.2 A desktop published story

well-defined end. Hypertexts, on the other hand, as explained in the previous chapter, are designed to be non-sequential. By using links the reader can navigate to different parts of the text and the sequence in which the text is read is determined by the reader. As we have seen, this makes a tremendous difference to the reader. There can be many sequences to the reading; there need not be one start to the text but several, and there need not be one ending. The reader is put in control of his/her own reading of the text to a greater extent, and passive reading is all but impossible. This active involvement with a text's shape and meaning blurs the traditional distinction between reader and writer, but it does, in turn, make the job of the reader more complex. Not only does the reader have to make active decisions about how to proceed through a hypertext (it is usually impossible to merely 'turn the pages'), but he/she also has to contend with a range of alternative textual material. Readers may be familiar with pictures and diagrams in traditional texts, but hypertexts, being computer-based, can also include segments of audio, video and other moving graphics, all of which contribute some extra potential meaning to a text.

If the reading of hypertexts poses extra problems for the reader, then the writing of successful hypertexts poses difficulties for the writer. But involving pupils in creating their own websites, for example, can significantly enhance their abilities to read critically and effectively the new texts they are presented with through ICT.

As a first step to this, many teachers offer pupils the chance to design and write their own web pages. Figure 10.3 shows the page designed by nine-year-old Marisa to show off her poem about winter. This page was designed in a specialised web page creation computer program and, in addition to the skills demanded in the writing of traditional text, it required Marisa to:

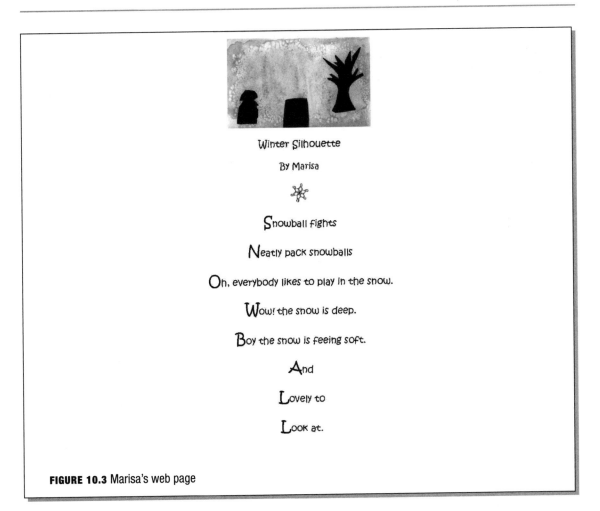

FIGURE 10.3 Marisa's web page

- scan and save her winter picture;
- embed this picture electronically within her poem;
- locate a snowflake picture and embed this within the poem;
- select a suitable font for her poem;
- decide on a layout for the poem and implement this within the software package; and
- publish her poem to her class website.

These are all complex skills and there are many adults, accomplished in other aspects of writing, who would not know how to do any of them.

But that is not all there is to website design which, principally, involves the creation of hypertexts. Like conventional writing, a hypertext requires planning. A collection of pages randomly linked together provides neither pleasure nor enlightenment for the reader. Nor will it allow the writer to transmit all his/her ideas fully to the reader. In planning a conventional essay, the writer builds a linear trail for the reader: the points should follow each other in a straight and logical line. But a genuine hypertext involves planning spatially, thinking about which pages (or parts of pages) should be linked to each other, or to external sources. A useful way of beginning to create this kind of text is to draft out on paper an outline of how the text might develop. Teachers can encourage pupils to do this graphically by drawing their main introductory screen in the middle of a large page, and then sketching out the subsidiary pages and indicating the links by arrows. They can then draw on a separate sheet the design for each page, as a story board.

Hypertext is a mixed medium. It can involve varying fonts, sizes and colours. It can also use graphic elements such as photographs, clip art, scanned drawings etc. Even more importantly, the writer needs to think about breaking up the page into blocks of text, each of which relates to other blocks, but which could, potentially, stand by itself.

In hypertext, writers compose small units of text and link them together. On the one hand, this eases the stress of writing, allowing the writer to work on discrete units, rather than a single long text. On the other hand, it means that hypertext writers need to pay particular attention to 'arrivals' and 'departures' – the first sentences their readers encounter in arriving at a text block and the last sentences they encounter as they leave. Each text block, of whatever length, needs to be shaped like a mini-essay, with a beginning, a middle and an end.

Reading a computer screen can be very distracting. The colours may be too bright, the background too distracting, the type may be too small, or it may be in such a continuous block that the eye loses its place on the screen. Hypertext writers need to choose restful, clear colours for their text and background. Writing is easier to read if it is broken up into small blocks, like in a newspaper.

The hypertext link is the equivalent of the TV's remote control. If readers get bored for a moment, they can instantly be somewhere else. Writers can combat this by thinking carefully about the links they include. Some include links only to the pages they have created themselves (many commercial organisations take this approach in their websites) but that ignores the potential of hypertext to link multiple sources of information.

A simple linking scheme is to give each page, or text block, a heading and to provide links to each of these at the bottom, or down the left-hand side, of each page. This allows the reader to get an overview of the entire document and then to select his/her own route through it.

This is not the place to give a full analysis of the difficulties of writing readable hypertext, but hopefully enough points have been raised in this section to suggest that this new medium for writing brings with it its own challenges and problems. Writing is no longer quite the same process, and in that fact lies much of the excitement of the new medium.

Conclusion

In this chapter I have tried to look at the potential of new technology from a writer's point of view. Writing with word-processors, desktop publishing and using hypertext all carry immense potential for writers to explore new ways of conveying their ideas. They also each bring new problems and it is the role of the teacher to begin to help learners solve these problems.

Conclusion

This has been yet another book about teaching literacy. There are plenty of others, as I explained in my introduction, but (I hope you will agree) not many cover exactly the same material I have covered here. The book has focused on the importance in literacy development of text and has covered issues such as: understanding and responding to fiction and non-fiction text; writing science and mathematics text; adopting a critical stance to text; and learning to handle new, electronic forms of text.

A crucial assumption I have made throughout the book is that by focusing upon text with our pupils, we naturally foreground meaning. Texts are meaningful artefacts: there would be little point in creating them if they meant nothing. We know how important meaning (I used the term 'authenticity' earlier) is to the development of literacy and focusing upon texts makes it possible for us to ensure that meaning is at the heart of the literacy work we do with pupils.

From their earliest experiences with literacy, most pupils will have picked up on the importance of texts and will have responded meaningfully to them. I will give a couple of examples of this only, both involving my own son.

We spent Alexander's third Christmas (he was two and a half years old) with some friends who have a son called Adam (then ten years old). The presents duly arrived under the tree and Christmas morning was spent in the traditional way, distributing and unwrapping the goodies. Alexander wanted to help in the present distribution, or rather he wanted to find his own presents, but that would involve some form of reading, or at least a recognition that his name began with A. We were impressed by the fact that this two and a half-year-old unfailingly managed to identify his own presents, but puzzled by seeing that he did not try to usurp any belonging to Adam. We eventually asked him how he knew that one of Adam's presents was not meant for him and he fixed us with a pitying glare before announcing that the name was too small! Here, then, was an example of urgent, meaningful literacy. Alexander had learnt that texts conveyed meaning and that there were clues in the text as to what that meaning was.

The second example I am almost ashamed to describe. As a rather older boy (around four), Alexander began to engage in one of his father's (rather childish) leisure pursuits – computer gaming. We would normally play together, with him on my knee and pressing one or two keys, while I did the difficult manoeuvring. Once, for some reason, I had to leave him alone for a few minutes to do something else. After a while, Alexander approached his mother with a piece of paper and asked her if she could write on the paper the words 'please god'. She was slightly puzzled but did as she was asked. A little later he came back, this time asking for the words 'please give all'. This time, his mother's curiosity became too much and she asked him why he wanted those words. The answer was obvious – these were the cheat codes which he had seen me enter into the computer lots of times (although I enjoy computer games, I'm never very good at them, and can't win unless I cheat!). The first gave his computer character infinite lives and the second infinite equipment.

Both these examples show what might be called 'urgent' literacy. Alexander is not unusual in that he has realised early in his life that there are many circumstances in which mastery of a text is highly significant. The order of importance here is also significant. In both cases, the need to achieve a socially desirable end came first, followed by the seeking of a relevant text, and finally attention to the details of that text.

What I have tried to suggest throughout this book is that this order of importance should also be used in the teaching of literacy in schools. Pupils need the big picture before the details will make sense. If the Literacy Strategy (or any other centrally driven literacy initiative) is to be truly successful in the long term in enhancing pupils' literacy, it needs to pay attention to this. Phonics, grammar, handwriting, spelling: they are all important, but only insofar as they enable pupils to read and write meaningful text more effectively.

References

Anderson, R., Wilson, P. and Fielding, L. (1983) 'Growth in reading and how children spend their time outside school'. *Reading Research Quarterly*, **23**, 285–303.

Austin, J. and Howson, A. (1979) 'Language and mathematics education'. *Educational Studies in Mathematics*, **10**, 161–97.

Borasi, R. and Rose, B. (1989) 'Journal writing and mathematics instruction'. *Educational Studies in Mathematics*, **20**, 347–65.

Brissenden, T. (1988) *Talking about Mathematics*. Oxford: Basil Blackwell.

Britton, J., Burgess, T., Martin, N., McLeod, A. and Rosen, H. (1975) *The Development of Writing Abilities (11–18)*. London: Macmillan.

Byrom, G. (1997) 'An evaluation of audio books as a resource for the failing reader'. Unpublished MEd. dissertation. Exeter: University of Exeter.

Cambourne, B. (1988) *The Whole Story*. Auckland, New Zealand: Ashton Scholastic.

Carbo, M. (1978) 'Teaching reading with talking books'. *The Reading Teacher*, **32**, 267–73.

Chambers, A. (1993) *Tell Me: Children, Reading and Talk*. Stroud: Thimble.

Chapman, J. (1983a) *Reading Development and Cohesion*. London: Heinemann.

Chapman, J. (1983b) 'A study in reading development: a comparison of the ability of 8-, 10- and 13-year-old children to perceive cohesion in their school texts', in Gillham, B. (ed.) *Reading through the Curriculum*. London: Heinemann.

Chapman, J. (1987) *Reading: From 5–11 Years*. Milton Keynes: Open University Press.

Christie, F. (1990) 'The changing face of literacy', in Christie, F. (ed.) *Literacy for a Changing World*. Hawthorn, Victoria: Australian Council for Educational Research.

Clarke, D., Waywood, A. and Stephens, M. (1993) 'Probing the structure of mathematical writing'. *Educational Studies in Mathematics*, **25**, 235–50.

Culler, J. (1981) *The Pursuit of Signs*. London: Routledge & Kegan Paul.

Daniel, D. B. and Reinking, D. (1987) 'The construct of legibility in electronic reading environments', in D. Reinking (ed.) *Reading and Computers: Issues for Theory and Practice*. New York: Teachers College Press, pp. 24–39.

Derewianka, B. (1990) (ed.) *Exploring How Texts Work*. Rozelle, New South Wales: Primary English Teaching Association.

Edwards, D. and Mercer, N. (1987) *Common Knowledge*. London: Methuen.

Eggleston, J., Galton, M. and Jones, M. (1976) *Processes and Products of Science Teaching*. London: Macmillan Education.

Emig, J. (1983) 'Writing as a mode of learning', in Goswami, D. and Butler, M. (eds) *The Web of Meaning: Essays on Writing, Teaching and Learning.* Upper Montclair, NJ: Boynton Cook, pp. 123–31.

Ervinck, G. (1992) 'Mathematics as a foreign language' in *Proceedings of the 16th Conference of the International Group for the Psychology of Mathematics Education (Volume 3).* Durham, NH: IGPME, pp. 217–33.

Freire, P. (1972) *Pedagogy of the Oppressed.* Harmondsworth: Penguin.

Gillman, L. (1987) *Writing Mathematics Well: A Manual for Authors.* The Mathematical Association of America.

Graves, D. (1983) *Writing: Teachers and Children at Work.* Portsmouth, NH: Heinemann.

Halliday, M. (1974) 'Some aspects of sociolinguistics', in *Interactions between Linguistics and Mathematical Education Symposium.* Paris: UNESCO.

Halliday, M. (1978) *Language as Social Semiotic.* London: Edward Arnold.

Halliday, M. and Hasan, R. (1976) *Cohesion in English.* London: Longman.

Halliday, M. and Hasan, R. (1989) *Language, Context and Text.* Oxford: Oxford University Press.

Haywood, S. and Wray, D. (1988) 'Using TRAY, a text reconstruction program, with top infants'. *Educational Review*, **40**, (1).

Johnston, V. (1985) 'Introducing the microcomputer into English: an evaluation of TRAY as a program using problem-solving as a strategy for developing reading skills'. *British Journal of Educational Technology*, **16**(3), 208–18.

Kane, R. (1968) 'The readability of mathematical English'. *Journal of Research in Science Teaching*, **5**, 296–8.

Knuth, D., Larrabee, T. and Roberts, P. (1989) *Mathematical Writing.* The Mathematical Association of America.

Konior, J. (1993) 'Research into the construction of mathematical texts'. *Educational Studies in Mathematics*, **24**, 251–6.

Krashen, S. (1993) *The Power of Reading.* Englewood, CO: Libraries Unlimited.

Kress, G. (1990) 'Two kinds of power'. *The English Magazine*, 24, 4–7.

Lemke, J. (1990) *Talking Science: Language, Learning and Values.* Norwood, NJ: Ablex.

Lewis, M. and Wray, D. (1997) *Writing Frames.* Reading: National Centre for Language and Literacy.

Lewis, M. and Wray, D. (1998) *Writing across the Curriculum.* Reading: University of Reading, Reading and Language Information Centre.

Littlefair, A. (1991) *Reading All Types of Writing.* Milton Keynes: Open University Press.

Lunin, L. R. and Rada, R. (1989) 'Hypertext: introduction and overview'. *Journal of the American Society for Information Science*, **40**, 159–63.

Marks, G. and Mousley, J. (1990) 'Mathematics, education and genre: dare we make the process writing mistake again?' *Language and Education*, **4**(2), 117–35.

Martin, J. (1989) *Factual Writing.* Oxford: Oxford University Press.

Martin, K. and Miller, E. (1988) 'Storytelling and science'. *Language Arts*, **65**(3), 255–9.

Martin, N., D'Arcy, P., Newton, B. and Parker, R. (1976) *Writing and Learning across the Curriculum 11–16.* London: Ward Lock.

Mason, J., Burton, L. and Stacey, K. (1985) *Thinking Mathematically.* Wokingham: Addison Wesley.

Mathematical Association (1987) *Maths Talk.* Cheltenham: Stanley Thornes.

Medwell, J. (1990) 'An investigation of the relationship between perceptions of the reading process and reading strategies of eight year old children'. Unpublished MEd. dissertation, University of Wales.

Medwell, J. (1991) 'Contexts for writing'. Paper given at the European Conference on Reading, Edinburgh, July.

Medwell, J. (1996) 'Talking books and reading'. *Reading*, **30**(1), 41–6.

Medwell, J. (1998) 'The talking books project: some further insights into the use of talking books to develop reading'. *Reading*, **32**(1), 3–9.

Meek, M. (1988) *How Texts Teach What Readers Learn* Stroud: Signal.

Morris, J. (1984) *Language in Action*. Basingstoke: Macmillan.

Osborne, J. and Collins, S. (2000) *Pupils' and Parents' Views of School Science*. London: King's College, University of London.

Pimm, D. (1987) *Speaking Mathematically: Communication in Mathematics Classrooms*. London: Routledge & Kegan Paul.

Reinking, D., and Rickman, S. S. (1990) 'The effects of computer-mediated texts on the vocabulary learning and comprehension of intermediate-grade readers'. *Journal of Reading Behavior*, **22**, 395–411.

Reinking, D. and Schreiner, R. (1985) 'The effects of computer-mediated text on measures of reading comprehension and reading behavior'. *Reading Research Quarterly*, **20**, 536–52.

Rogers, A. and MacDonald, C. (1985) *Teaching Writing for Learning*. Edinburgh: Scottish Council for Research in Education.

Rosenblatt, L. (1978) *The Reader, The Text, The Poem*. Carbondale: Southern Illinois University Press.

Rumelhart, D. (1985) 'Toward an interactive model of reading', in Singer, H. and Ruddell, R. (eds) *Theoretical Models and Processes of Reading*. Newark, DE: International Reading Association.

Searle, C. (1998) *None but Our Words*. Buckingham: Open University Press.

Shor, I. (1992) *Empowering Education: Critical Teaching for Social Change*. Chicago: University of Chicago Press.

Shuard, H. and Rothery, A. (1984) *Children Reading Mathematics*. London: Murray.

Topping, K., Shaw, M. and Bircham, A. (1997) 'Family electronic literacy: part 1 – Home–school links through audiotaped books'. *Reading*, **31**(2), 7–11.

Williams, K. M. (2003) 'Writing about the problem-solving process to improve problem-solving performance'. *Mathematics Teacher*, **96**(3), 185–7.

Wray, D. (1994) *Literacy and Awareness*. London: Hodder & Stoughton.

Wray, D. (2002) *Practical Ways to Teach Writing*. Reading: National Centre for Language and Literacy.

Wray, D., Bloom, W. and Hall, N. (1989) *Literacy in Action*. Lewes: Falmer Press.

Wray, D. and Lewis, M. (1992) 'Primary children's use of information books'. *Reading*, **26**(3), 19–24.

Wray, D. and Lewis, M. (1997) *Extending Literacy*. London: Routledge.

Wray, D. and Medwell, J. (2003) *Easiteach Literacy: Content Pack*. Abingdon: Research Machines.

Wray, D., Medwell, J., Poulson, L. and Fox, R. (2002) *Teaching Literacy Effectively*. London: RoutledgeFalmer.

Index